AFRICA OR DEATH

AFRICA
or
DEATH

by

Rev. A. G. Mondini, F.S.C.J.

A Biography of Bishop Daniel Comboni
Founder of the Missionary Societies of
The Verona Fathers (Sons S.H.)
and
The Verona Sisters

ST. PAUL EDITIONS

NIHIL OBSTAT:

SHAWN G. SHEEHAN
Diocesan Censor

IMPRIMATUR:

✠ RICHARD CARDINAL CUSHING
Archbishop of Boston

Library of Congress Catalog Card Number: 64-22431

To All My
Young
Fellow
Americans
and
To the Martyrs
of
Southern Sudan

ACKNOWLEDGMENT

To all my young friends, who helped so generously, my cordial thanks.

To Sr. Mary Simplicia, I.H.M., Dean, English Department, St. Mary's College, Monroe, Michigan, for her invaluable help and encouragement, no words I can find to express my gratitude.

CONTENTS

GOLDEN DAWN   (1831-1857)

THE IMPOSSIBLE   (1857-1872)

SCARLET SUNSET   (1872-1881)

CUT FLOWERS

14

1

GOLDEN DAWN

1831 - 1857

AFRICA, AFRICA

Verona, October 10, 1881. Evening. Young Sister Matilde Corsi is praying in her cell. The two small missionary communities of priests and sisters for Africa, founded some ten years before by Bishop Comboni, are passing long hours in prayer and offering extraordinary mortifications for their beloved Founder and the Missions. From Khartoum lately they received only alarming news.

It is late at night but the young Sister keeps on praying. Suddenly it seems that heaven opens before her eyes and she can see angels and saints extraordinarily happy, waiting for a "great soul who is due there at any moment." After this extraordinary experience she is not afraid, only she wishes she could explain the meaning, if any, of the "strange thing."

Some days later when the news of the death of the Venerable Founder and Father reached Verona, Sister Matilde exclaimed: "Now I know whose soul heaven was waiting for." [1]

It was exactly 10 P.M., October 10, 1881, when Bishop Daniel Comboni passed away in Khartoum, capital of the Sudan.

[1] The Sister testified the happening under oath in the ordinary investigation for Comboni's cause. She died in 1930. During her very long stay in Africa she administered over 18,000 Baptisms, almost all *in articulo mortis*. Sister Matilde was called the "grandmother of the Africans."

17

He was born in Limone, Italy, March 15, 1831.

At the end of high school I was taken to Limone as a graduation gift. While the bus was zooming through the tunnels of the beautiful Riviera of Lake Garda, the ever changing and enchanting scenery could not efface from my mind a silly question: "Why under the sun did they call a town 'Lemon'—'Limone' in Italian—?" I was glad I was prudent enough not to manifest my problem to anyone because as soon as we arrived there the answer was self-evident. The tiny village in those good old times must have looked like one huge green house of lemons. Although the main frames were pretty much gone to pieces, many smart white little columns were still there to help the visitor reconstruct mentally the beauty of the past.

Many of the houses today remain—as they were—bathing in the blue Garda, while others are progressively going away from it, disorderly, uphill.

About a mile or so from the village, right under the rough, broken cliff and buried in the dark green olives are a few houses named Teseul. One of these belonged to the Comboni's. The place is exceptionally peaceful and inviting. On the other side of the projecting rock, a small, noisy waterfall adds to the whole a note of freshness and gaiety.

Louis Comboni and Domenica Pace-Comboni were ordinary working people. They had eight children of whom Daniel was the fourth. The spiritual atmosphere of the family was exactly like the one described by Pope John when in June, 1962 he spoke at the first International Congress on Priestly Vocations. Love for God was the supreme law. Family life centered around the Church, the Pastor being the beloved father of all, whose authority was unconditionally accepted in everything with veneration.

Long before school age little Daniel was going to church daily. A companion of his childhood remembered how he used to kneel down all alone, his hands folded on his breast and say the usual morning prayers his mother had taught him. The same companion could never forget a very significant detail: "Daniel loved to pray at the altar of the Blessed Mother and when the priest or the catechist talked of her, or only mentioned her name, we could see him smile, filled with joy."

The happy memories of the old folks of Limone go even farther back in Daniel's life. At sunset, coming from work and passing by the Teseul, how many times they saw the tiny boy standing with arms wide open over a little chair, or on a rock and preaching, preaching, preaching, heavens only knew what. Two words, however, used to come out very often and distinctly: "Africa, Africa." The relatives down to the last neighbor could only shake their heads and laugh. What on earth he meant only God could know!

And God apparently did know.

NATURE AND GRACE TOGETHER

"Mom, Daddy, I want to be a priest." It was the fall of 1841 and Daniel was ten years old.

The good parents were very pleased, but not surprised when their child revealed his secret to them. Daniel was, in a way, so much a real boy and yet he seemed so different from the others.

Teacher Susio taught him everything he could under the circumstances in the first four years of grade school. Then he was obliged to give him up when the rest of the pupils "just could not follow" and were left too far behind.

In the long afternoons of the good seasons no one except Daniel seemed able to keep together such a large crowd of boys, playing hide and seek on the beautiful hills of the Teseul, behind rocks and bushes and under the dark-green olive trees. Not a fight, not a quarrel. At times the playing went on until dusk when the voice of a mother echoed from the hills calling for home. Then the group dispersed quietly, to the repeated refrain of: "See you tomorrow, boys. Bye, Daniel."

A recurring mystery for Papa Louis was the way the little spending money disappeared from Daniel's pockets. He confided the problem to his brother Joseph. Uncle Joe was one of those men who are born police. "I will find out for you, and soon!" he smiled to his brother. That Sunday afternoon before Vespers a Catechism contest of the children was to be held in church before the whole congregation. Uncle Joe was positive that Daniel would be there long before the crowd gathered in the church square talking and joking while waiting for the last bell, to go in. Neither did he have any doubt that the explanation of the disappearing money lay in the fruit stand opposite the church door in the little square. Accordingly, he was there two hours early, in a nice little corner behind a pillar ready for the "ambush" and smilingly confident of his plans. Not long after he heard the familiar voice. And then Daniel appeared followed by one, two, three . . . five, six other little boys. As they lined up along the fruit stand, Uncle Joe's smile died on his lips. What next now? All got what they wanted and Daniel called for the bill. "Oh no!" growled Uncle Joe coming out into the open. "Hi, Uncle Joe!" said Daniel smiling. "Come on, boys, all to Catechism now."

The good old priest cut Catechism very short for the adults that Sunday afternoon and invited them all to stay for the children's Catechism contest. "You will see what your children know and what they don't know. You are very much aware of how holy Mother Church ardently insists on the teaching of Christian doctrine. And of course parents cannot be kept absent from it. After all, the responsibility is yours first."

The children, led by their Catechists, started to file into the church group by group, orderly and in silence, the boys first.

When the old pastor from his "Cathedra" opened with the first question, the packed church was wrapped in a dead silence, the tension visible in most parents' faces. Wonderful, unforgettable memories of childhood! In this intense parish life, so family-like, generous vocations thrive.

The good pastor dispensed from Vespers that afternoon and the contest closed with Benediction of the most Blessed Sacrament.

Many a parent, coming out of the church, stopped to congratulate Daniel's mother and father: "That boy of yours!"—"And how he can lead his group!"

Daniel loved to sing too. He was singing all the time: around the house, going to school, alone in the orchard yard, or with a crowd of boys under a tree up in the hills. But his favorite singing was for God. He literally enjoyed singing Vespers on Sunday afternoon with his pastor and the congregation. That large crowd singing for almost an hour with all their heart and might had an electrifying effect on the young boy. He felt so relaxed and satisfied afterwards. Indeed it was for him the very best way to give vent to all the warmth of his heart for God. Never, never once for anything did he miss Vespers on Sunday afternoon.

Naturally, little Daniel was an altar boy from the time he was big enough to carry the huge old missal around the altar. His pastor expressly wanted him at the altar and Daniel easily learned the answers of the Mass in Latin. In all his Missionary life languages were never once a problem for him.

Like many boys of his age, he had his own little altar to the beloved Madonna where he used to gather his small neighbors. Unlike other boys, however, Daniel used to ring a bell and swing a stick to round them up for Marian devotions. We can excuse, of course, even if we cannot approve these too convincing methods with his little friends who willing or not had no other choice than to obey.

"What will you do with this boy?" Uncle Joe asked Papa Louis one day. "We would rather put the question this way: 'What will God do with this boy?'"

VERONA

"Please, Daddy, stay here with me!" and leaping into his father's arms, Daniel burst into tears.

It was easy to convince the brave, little missionary, however, that Papa Louis had to go home to work, and that Daniel had to stay in Verona to study hard if he really wanted to be a priest.

Back in Limone the good father had to console Mamma Domenica who anxiously assailed him with all kinds of questions. "Are you sure he has enough to eat? Is his bed comfortable? Do they like him down there? Do you think he's going to stay? Did he cry when you left? Oh, Blessed Mother, he is all yours, yes, but why so soon?"

"All right! You start crying too now!" said the poor man, going outdoors to hide his own emotion.

During his first year in Verona, Daniel boarded at the Ranbottini's, a good old couple but rather poor. They were very kind to him, but more than once the child did not have enough to eat. He never complained, however, when his father came to visit him; neither did he ever write a word about it in his letters to his mother. That would have meant suffering distress for both his parents and the old couple. And that he could never do. Already this ten-year old seemed to have so clearly outlined in his soul that typical trait which was the unmistakable mark of his whole life: he could not see people suffer; he would willingly give anything, even his own life to spare a tear, to relieve sorrow wherever it was to be found. This feature implanted in his nature by God will be transformed by grace into an all-powerful passion which will make of him the hero of the Dark Continent, the savior of a race lost to mankind.

Far away from his dear parish and beloved pastor, Daniel's love for prayer and enthusiasm for God and Church did not diminish. He soon joined the "Oratorio" of St. James attached to the Cathedral, where he could pass all Sundays and Holydays alternating playing with Mass, Catechism and afternoon devotions under the supervision of the assistant priests and Catholic Action members. It was almost like being back at Limone again. New companions, true, new priests and leaders, different places and things, but the same parochial organizations, the same spirit, the same love.

Between school, church, and oratorio activities, time passed quickly. The "Great Day" for Daniel was now approaching. Everyone, and the young priest of the Oratorio above all, had the chance to know very soon and appreciate the beauty of the soul of the little boy from Limone. When the list of the First Communion class was made up, his name was among the first ones. When informed of the big news, he was overcome with joy and started a preparation all of his own. It seems that never in Comboni's life was anything important ever done in a common way. His great heart, unconditionally kept for God and his heavenly Mother, always went all out with a unique warmth for God and God's cause. His first reception of Jesus in Holy Communion could never be compared with anything else, in his whole life. Overcome with emotion he said out loud in tears: "God to me, God to me ..." It was then that the youngster from the green hills of Lake Garda offered himself generously to his Divine Master. If He wanted, his life was at His disposal for anything, anywhere, forever.

And God took him at his word.

A TEENAGER

In November, 1842, Daniel was accepted as a day student in the high school of the diocesan seminary of Verona. It was at this time that Papa Louis discovered the difficulties Daniel was having, food-wise, at the Ranbottini's. Obliged to speak, Daniel, of course, could not lie, so his father took him away. But where to put him now? Mr. Louis Comboni was no rich man, but Divine Providence again was going to provide.

In 1832 Father Nicholas Mazza opened a private school in Verona for students with no financial means. All the saintly priest required from the boys was a good mind a little over the average and good morals. No fees. Perfect freedom for the boys to choose the vocation they liked. The young Daniel joined Father Mazza's children on February, 1843. Under the warmth of the great educator, the generous lad from the hills of Limone developed beautifully in soul and mind. Always generous, always first. Grace found the real cast for heroic things in a gifted nature which most definitely remained on the "hot" side. We know grace does not destroy nature: just works on it.

Verona, summer 1848. It is a Thursday afternoon and just outside the walls, beyond St. George's

gate, a furious ball game is on between the best two
teams of Verona: Mazza High *versus* Accoliti High.
The score is tied, time is running out and the impa-
tient crowd is getting excited and more noisy by the
minute. The heat is terrific. The players' faces are
red hot and covered with sweat and dirt; their tension and nervousness is reaching the climax. Both
teams want to break the tie, yet neither is resigned
to lose, and, to end in a draw sounds simply ridiculous to the young players. Even the Austrian sentry
on the Bastion stops pacing, and looks on apparently
amused. Really something has to happen!

Two, three idle passages and Daniel gets the
ball at last. The thing now must really happen.
Knowing very well that he is the one who can do
it, the crowd is accompanying his action with thunderous: "Come on, Dan, Come on, boy..." Daniel
very cautiously is approaching his foes' goal, his
speed keeps increasing. He easily avoids one opponent, dribbles to another one, bravely fools a
third and the way is clear. Only the left-back is
interfering a little but Daniel avoids him by aiming
at the right corner of the goal. Unfortunately, in doing so, his tremendous kick deviates, the ball hits
like a bomb the transversal pole, bounces up high
in the air, and lands on the Bastion, a few feet from
the Austrian sentry. The crowd has stopped yelling
and Daniel, always racing, is there at the foot of the
slope begging the sentry for the ball. The soldier
scornfully pretends not to hear. Daniel offers him a

reward, but to no avail. Finally, the sentry with his gun's bayonette pierces the ball raising it up in the air. The crowd explodes in rage, aiming its fists at the Austrian. Daniel, who has disappeared for a moment, is up there now face to face with the soldier. The crowd is tensely silent. Apparently a few words are exchanged between the two, which nobody down below can understand. Suddenly all those faces looking up see the young lad jump on the soldier, take and throw away his gun and roll him down into the ditch. A roar accompanied the flashing action. Then Daniel rejoined his team. The crowd dispersed. For a few days Verona spoke with excitement of ball games, brave young men and Austrian sentries.

AND PEACHES

At times people wonder how collossal works of charity can go on without any definite source of funds.

Divine Providence is the only answer. God never fails, although He does sometimes try his faithful servants. The St. Charles College founded by Father Mazza had its dark days. There was a time when food had to be rationed and it is quite hard of course to reason with the stomachs of growing boys.

It is around four in the afternoon and the students are getting ready to go out for the customary walk. Divided in groups they all file before Father Rector who looks at each one carefully and does not hesitate to send back anyone whose appearance is not quite satisfactory.

Naturally, when passing before Father, all take their hats off. All but Daniel who walks with eyes to the floor as one who is far away in his thoughts. The thing is rather strange and the good rector calls the attention of the boy, but to no avail. That is rather too much. "Hey boy, where are you going?"

At the voice of the Superior, the entire group halts. Daniel's face gets terribly red, but he does not utter a word. Some of the boys start giggling. The Rector becomes really suspicious and he thunders: "Did you hear me?"

A few, long seconds of dead silence follow. Finally, Daniel mumbling something, starts raising up his top hat slowly, hesitatingly, with both hands. At that point one peach falls down from under it, then two, then over half a dozen. The action is accompanied by a roar from the boys. The terrible rector is trying hard to bite his lips but cannot refrain from smiling.

What had happened. That very morning a carload of peaches had been purchased and stored in the cellar. Some of the boys who suffered more from the food rationing had used the occasion to help themselves. Among them was Daniel, who planned to share his peaches with others, but who had the unhappy idea of hiding them in such an unsafe place.

Heroes and saints don't rain down from heaven. They are just common human beings. But somehow, someday, they decide not to live a cheap common life.

VACATION TIME

At the end of the school year Daniel was glad to return to his Limone. He was deeply in love with his enchanting blue Garda, its green hills scented with lemons and oranges. He could stand there for hours just looking. His lungs eagerly breathed the oxygen-rich, life-giving air. His virgin soul, satiated with beauty all soaked in God.

In the small village, up in the mountains, life is lived almost in common, family-like. Of great concern to everybody are particularly the sick. In spite of a tiring long day of work, it seems natural to men and particularly women to stay up all night at the bedside of a sick neighbor. Daniel loved that. During the summer vacations he literally took charge of them. Never did he feel so close to God as when serving the sick and helping the needy. He not only used to give his little money to the poor, but in unexpected urgent cases he even gave away some of the very clothes he was wearing. Many instances of this kind are still remembered in Limone.

Moreover, it was not rare that Papa Louis had his family increased by two instead of one during the summer vacations. Daniel knew all his companions at St. Charles very well. Nobody could have any secret with him. He knew for certain that some were much poorer than himself. Therefore, with the excuse that he would feel lonesome all summer alone, he almost forced some of them to visit him. And he kept them as long as he could.

His father felt obliged at times to remind him that after all he was not rich either. Daniel used to answer entreatingly: "Oh Pop, they are such good boys and they are so poor. God will provide for us."

During the school year, but particularly in summer-time, Daniel loved to read the lives of the Saints. Somehow, at this age, he was very impressed by the example of the Monks and hermits of old. The idea of eating grass and wild fruits, of drinking water from the spring in the valley, of living in a cave and sleeping on the ground was really something thrilling. He was going to do the same: to say good-bye to the world and live all and only for God.

In fact, more than once he left for the mountains that protect Limone all around and keep it down close to the lake. His determination was sincere and everything was fine till the sun started to go down. Then he invariably concluded that, all in all, it was safer to go home. To his mother who anxiously was asking him where he could have been all day without food he only answered, "Oh, just somewhere up there. Really, Mother, I did not feel too hungry."

But one day he felt ashamed of all that baby stuff of being afraid to stay alone at night, and his parents did not see him home for supper. At dusk his mother could not wait any longer and she went to all the neighbors looking for him. But no one had seen him all day. The desolate mother was almost out of her mind. He never did anything like that before, something must have happened to him.

His father was not less worried, but not knowing what else to do, he tried to hide his feelings and quiet down his wife, "Nothing to worry about. He has been going up there often lately. And certainly he knows that mountain better than you and I. Let's go to rest!"

But neither parent could sleep all that night. In the morning the hermit-to-be was easily found and this was the last adventure of this kind for Daniel.

BACK TO SCHOOL

Daniel loved to learn. He made all his studies with the boys of Father Mazza at the diocesan seminary in Verona. In high school, and later, in philosophy and theology, he was always among the first. His memory was extraordinary. He could name, for example, all the Roman emperors from the first till the very last of the Holy Roman Empire, straight, one after the other without missing one. He was especially gifted in learning languages. He also liked music and knew how to play the piano.

One of his companions, Monsignor Stegagnini, remembered how Daniel was one of the most popular boys in the whole seminary.

But the saintly Father Mazza was discovering qualities far more important in the brilliant young man from Limone. He could read Daniel's soul as an open book. It was no secret to him that the innocence of heart the little boy brought to Verona, years before, was never lost. He closely followed with delight his daily efforts to improve. But above all he was most evidently witnessing in his dear son an exceptionally great heart. He could suffer anything, he could forgive anything.

Although nobody ever found out why, but probably because of envy, one day a school companion unexpectedly attacked him with a knife. It was in a corner of the stairs going up to the second floor and the coward attacker took care that no one was around.

Although Daniel could rather easily defend himself, his right hand was bleeding when he came down to the refectory. The boys seeing him a little excited with a handkerchief around his hand anxiously assailed him with all kinds of questions.

He simply said: "That poor fellow tried to hurt me!"

But no matter how much they insisted on learning the name of the "poor fellow" and other details, they could get nowhere. Daniel invariably repeated: "Forget about it! It's all over!" He most resolutely refused any medication and insistently pleaded "to drop the case," because it was "really nothing!"

Many, many years later when viciously attacked by serpentine tongues trying to kill him morally before the Pope and the world, he not only forgave in his usual way but was able to add: "I will always pray for those who made me suffer so much. They don't know, they mean well."

Indeed it was hard, not to say impossible, to think they meant well. But that only Comboni could do.

GOD CALLS

Despite its poverty and simplicity, Father Mazza's previous institution for boys had just about everything useful to help them develop their good qualities and inclinations. Among other things was a library.

Daniel was a terrific reader. Second to books that complemented his studies, his preference was for the adventurous, the extraordinary. One day he happened to see a book by the title: "History of the Japanese Martyrs." It sounded different and appealing. He read it all in a breath and that was it! He was going to be a missionary, sail to Japan and, God willing, die for his faith. He was fifteen now and he certainly thought he knew what he was doing.

At last he seemed to have a purpose in life. His prayers became more fervent, his ways more thoughtful and considerate. The ardent desire of his heart had found an adequate object.

But too often man's plans are not exactly God's.

Three years later, during January, 1849, Father Angelo Vinco, an ex-alumnus of St. Charles, came to visit Father Mazza's boys. Back from Central Africa, he was in Verona to solicit funds for the newly-opened mission and particularly to rouse in-

terest and possibly generous vocations among the
young students. The colorful description of that unknown country packed with adventure and dangers
of all kinds; the horrible conditions of the natives,
slaves both of Satan and of men; the absolute absence of any sign of civilization and comforts; the
murderous climate, everything was just what a hand-
ful of generous young men were waiting for. They
all got together one day and went to see Father
Mazza. The old man with tears in his eyes, promised
them to try anything possible to satisfy their desires,
God willing.

Daniel Comboni was naturally in the group. He
could see now in a more concrete manner what
missionary life looked like. There was not a doubt
any more in his mind: the African race was the most
unfortunate of all, so for it his life shall be spent.
"I will be a missionary in Central Africa!"

He was beginning now—in 1850—his theological
courses, and the Sacred Studies vastly helped his
soul and mind which now were most definitely ori-
ented towards sanctity.

He understood even better now that ordinary
virtue is not quite enough for missionary life. Extreme difficulties call for corresponding heroism.
So his interior life became more solid and deep; he
worked hard to smooth the impetuosity of his character; very diligently he channeled the powerful forces
of his heart towards God alone.

To discipline his body he cut down on food and sleep, trying to accustom it to privations and hardships. He dedicated more time to the study of languages and also of some medicine.

But above all he devoted himself more to prayer and intense meditation. His love for the Mother of God at this time reached its maturity.

PRIEST FOREVER

At the beginning of September, 1854, Daniel was unanimously admitted by his superiors to the Major Orders. December 10, he was ordained sub-deacon; December 17, deacon, and December 31, priest. All three major orders were given to him by the venerable John Nepomucen, Bishop of Trent.

The dream of his first Communion day had come true and the first great goal of his life was attained. With the Divine Victim he offered himself unconditionally for the redemption of Central Africa. Now it was only a matter of time.

Great celebrations at Limone were prepared for the beloved son. The narrow street leading from the little harbor on the Lake Garda to the church was beautifully decorated with colorful arches of flowers and evergreens. Every house had festoons of every kind hanging from the windows and around the doors. It was quite evident that the little mountain village was all out with its unmatched cordiality and spontaneity to make the celebration a real triumph.

The church already at its utmost for the Christmas holidays seemed even more solemn and devout.

When the young priest at Communion time left the altar to come down to give Jesus to his parents, many in the packed church were in tears.

But probably the emotion reached its climax in the afternoon, when, after Vespers, Father Daniel briefly addressed the congregation. He thanked first his mother and father and the dear old pastor and after, one by one, all the different groups and organizations. His clear voice, his fluency of speech and perfect self-control kept all, young and old alike, hanging on his lips from the first word to the last.

The good people made the most enthusiastic remarks about the "famous" sermon. Invariably everyone recalled how the little Daniel used to preach up there at the Teseul, many, many years back.

"That's it", commented the old folks in one accord. "We always said it! This young man is going to be one of the greatest speakers of all times!" "Vox populi. . ." "Voice of the people, voice of God!"

Back at Verona, Father Daniel was sure to find something more definite about the new mission in Central Africa that saintly Father Mazza had obtained from the Sacred Congregation of Propaganda Fide. But things were not quite ready yet. However, God did not allow him to waste any precious time.

1855, SUMMER DRILL

The cholera morbus was hitting hard at Verona and the neighboring villages for the third time in succession.

With some other confreres, Father Daniel offered himself to the Bishop to be sent wherever help was needed.

The very same day he set out for and reached his destination, Buttapietra. There he found the old pastor and the people in terror and for some six months he became all to all.

Day and night, close by or far away in the country, with food or without, "he was everywhere like the mercy and love of God," people used to say. He felt he belonged to his parishioners and they had the right to call on him anytime for anything.

In such a predicament, doctors are always too scarce, and so many a time Father Daniel took the doctor's place. He was studying medicine for his future mission in Africa and God was so good in giving him a chance to start practicing it here at home. Besides being priest, nurse, and doctor, quite often he was undertaker too.

In order to answer any night call more quickly, he used to take a little rest on a bench with his clothes on. His generosity did not know restrictions. One time he happened to be urgently called by a very poor family. In no time he was at the bedside of the sick, but being completely out of any kind of bandages, he asked if, by chance, they had a piece of clean linen. The poor people looked at each other feeling embarrassed. Father Daniel pretended not to understand and immediately added: "That's all right! Just a moment please." He dashed into the adjacent room and in a minute he was back with a nice piece of white linen. Later, when the house-keeper was doing the washing she was surprised to see one of the assistant's shirts without a sleeve and naturally she asked him what happened. "Oh, nothing!" said Father Daniel smiling.

"Nothing?" repeated the old lady, her eyes and and mouth wide open.

"Yes . . . you know how it is . . . . Sometimes you are out to see the sick and you urgently need some kind of bandage and you don't have it, and . . . you know . . ."

"Heavens above! and you mean you used your shirt for that!? . . ."

But the old lady kept the shirt and when the plague was over she used to show it to the people who came to the rectory. After telling them the story in her lively manner she invariably commented: "See what I mean? Our young priest was a saint."

One night Father Daniel laid his purse on the table of the sick person he was visiting and

left it there. At least he said he forgot it. When
he returned in the morning the money was all gone.
Father Daniel took the empty purse in his right
hand and pretending to weigh it said laughingly: "I
like it this way; easy to carry!" And taking his left
hand out of his pocket he distributed the little
change he had to the children.

Each family had a story of its own to tell.
All were thanking and blessing God for having
sent them the young priest from Verona like an angel from heaven during their terrible trials.

When it was all over Father Daniel left, but
the good people of Buttapietra kept him in their
hearts.

THE STAR DISAPPEARS

Like a soldier after tough military maneuvers Father Daniel came back to Verona ready and more eager than ever for action. The desire for Africa had become almost an obsession. There was even a time when he felt that a longer delay was going to drive him out of his mind. But Father Mazza convinced him that the will of God was to wait and so he waited. Almost two long, interminable years passed during which Father Daniel offered up each single day for the salvation of that unfortunate continent which in all truth was the only reason for his existence for the rest of his life.

Meanwhile, Father Mazza was not wasting time, by any means! Elementary prudence demanded an extremely diligent preparation. It appeared more evident every day that the Mission of Central Africa was one of the most challenging adventures the Church had ever undertaken.

The first mission founded in Khartoum on May 20, 1842 by the Lazarists' Father Montuory did not last much over two years. Young Father Serrao who took his place could not get used to the horrible climate of Khartoum and went back to Europe. Blessed De Jacobis, prefect Apostolic of

Ethiopia, mentioning the departure of his missionary wrote: "The young man was not able to stand any longer that *inferno* of Sennaar!"

On April 3, 1846, Pope Gregory XVI erected the new Vicariate of Central Africa.[1] Father Casolani was consecrated bishop to direct it. Father Ryllo, S. J., Father Pedemonte, S. J., Father Ignatius Knoblecher, and Father Angelo Vinco were assigned to the new mission. Following the almost immediate resignation of Bishop Casolani, Father Ryllo took over as Pro-Vicar Apostolic. The four missionaries arrived in Khartoum, February, 1848, and Father Ryllo died the following June. Father Knoblecher succeeded him as Pro-Vicar. The new mission was encountering all kinds of difficulties.

Meanwhile, Father Vinco had returned to Europe for help where we saw him in Verona at St. Charles as the instrument used by Divine Providence to set on fire Father Mazza and his boys for Central Africa.

But now Father Vinco also was dead. He had returned to Khartoum in the heart of the dark continent, February, 1851. In Libo, among the Bari tribe, he built his hut and worked all alone till 1853. When in January of the same year Father Knoblecher arrived in Libo with other missionaries on

[1] It was the largest in the world. Its borders were: *North*: Egypt, Lybia, Tunisia, Algeria; *South*: the Mountain of the Moon, (the Mountain chain of the Ruwerzori); *East*: the Red Sea and Abyssinia; *West*: the two Guineas and the Sahara.

the new boat "Morning Star", Father Vinco was
very sick. After receiving the last sacraments, he
died in the arms of his confreres, January 22, 1853.
Vinco's was the first cross on the White Nile, he was
the first martyr of Father Mazza's family.

The sad news did not discourage the old man's
great heart. He just had to be more cautious. Before
exposing his boys he was going to try anything prudence could suggest. Therefore, a few months after
the death of Vinco, he sent two of his priests, Beltrame and Castagnaro, to Khartoum to talk things
over with Pro-Vicar Knoblecher and explore with
him a suitable place for a new mission. But a few
months later, February, 1854, Father Castagnaro
was dying at Khartoum.

Father Beltrame, however, was back in Verona
one year later, with at least one bit of good news:
Knoblecher was waiting for them any time they
felt ready.

Preparations for the great enterprise were even
accelerated, but still it took about two years, as we
have said, before Father Mazzza could set a tenta-
tive date for the departure. It is impossible to describe the commotion the big news provoked at
St. Charles.

Now at this point of Father Daniel's life, something strange happened, something that we often
read about in the lives of the saints. He had waited
so impatiently for this day. How many times he had
gone to Father Mazza asking him about Africa and

pleading with him, please, to hurry. He had passed these two years studying hard and preaching in different parishes of the diocese, but even the most active life could not lessen much the torture of the long waiting. Now the big news had come, and instead of being out of himself with joy, a cruel doubt had clung to his soul.

"Was he worthy of such a sublime vocation? Did God really call him? Perhaps all his frenzy was nothing but a crazy fever for adventure. A work of a hot, unbalanced head."

Heaven was closed. Even the Mother of God seemed to have disappeared from his soul.

Some twenty-four years later Father Daniel would recall in every detail this turning point in his life. "I entered the room of my spiriual director, Father Marani, half dead. A question kept hammering in my poor head: What if Father says that I'm not fit for Africa? My God, what am I going to do then?"

And Father Daniel will also always remember the answer of Father Marani that he considered from God Himself, "I have known you since you were a student. You always came to me for advice in all your problems. I can clearly see all your life as in a mirror. I know all your good points, your defects, and what you have done to correct them. I have been examining vocations of all kinds since 1820. I can frankly tell you before God that your

vocation for the African missions is one of the clear-
est I have ever seen. . . . Go in peace and good luck
to you. . ."

"I fell at his feet," Father Daniel wrote, "and
the old man blessed me. I was immensely happy
and in tears."

The star of his vocation reappeared higher and
brighter than ever. If at times almost superhuman
obstacles were met by our missionary with the
granitic determination that amazed all, it was due
to the "oracle" of Father Marani. Daniel Comboni
himself will suggest this again and again. It seems
very logical, as one of his biographers says, to think
that his all-famous war cry "Africa or Death" was
more clearly formulated at this time, or at least never
before pronounced by him more forcefully. God
wants it. Nothing ever will stop him! "Africa or
Death!"

"MAMMA DOMENICA"

It was early in the morning, that summer of 1857. Comboni would never forget it. The first light of the day was chasing a lazy moon fading away in a corner of the sky. The morning chorus of many birds was in full crescendo. Close by the house, on the large oak, a nightingale had already begun his ninety-nine songs. From far away in the tall, slim poplars came the timid cooing of a dove.

The three were walking one behind the other: Father Daniel leading, then his mother and then his father.

Nobody was talking. Their minds were too pre-occupied even to notice the acute, delicate perfume of the lemon trees, loaded with flowers and fruits. Father Daniel was home to say good-bye before sailing for Africa. His dearest parents were far from being young anymore. And they were poor. But above all, they were all alone. Of the eight children God gave them, six had passed away in their childhood and one at twenty-one. Daniel was actually their only son and their very life.

The old father gave him his consent in tears but without difficulty. Mamma Domenica just couldn't. She felt something so powerfully strange overcoming her. Vaguely but deeply in her heart she sensed that she was never going to see him again. Oh, so seldom do mothers make a mistake! Daniel, who was trying to keep smiling, had agony in his heart. Before coming home he had written two letters to his Pastor begging him to prepare his most loved ones for the heart-breaking departure. "Oh, how the sacrifice of my adorable parents is torturing me! With such terrible tests is God trying my vocation! But He has spoken and I will go. I know that many, who don't see an inch beyond their nose, will condemn and perhaps curse my decision. But I will never for that betray my vocation. My only hope is God, the Immaculate Virgin and your good heart, dear father. I know Heaven will recompense you."

And the good Pastor had tried, but not with much success. As a last expedient, Daniel had proposed to throw the whole affair into the Blessed Mother's lap. The three would get up early in the morning and go to Church where he would offer the Holy Sacrifice at the Altar of the Mediatrix of all graces. They would receive Holy Communion and pray for the will of God, whatever it might be.

All three got in church together, but Mamma Domenica was very soon back at the church door helping with holy water those who were coming in and whispering to everyone, "Please, tell the Blessed Mother to keep my Daniel home."

But the Blessed Mother decided otherwise and good Mamma Domenica bowed to her will.

September, 1857, had already begun and Daniel was rather late. From the deck of the steamboat anchored on the dark blue Garda he was now giving his farewell to the disconsolate mother, his father, his Pastor and to all Limone who had come out to see him maybe for the last time.

The whistle of the boat pierced sharply through Daniel's heart. A jolt and he was cut off from the land of his birth, of his love. He kept waving till the people, the little harbor and the houses were out of sight. Then he sat down: "Now, O Lord, I am at your orders, Africa or Death!" And he realized he was weeping.

From Verona he sent his picture to Mom and Dad. He had written behind it: "Who loves father and mother more than Me, is not worthy of Me."

They say that Mamma Domenica, covering the precious gift with kisses and tears, had exclaimed: "God gave me eight children and here I am now with only one on paper."

She never saw her Daniel here on earth anymore. But her sacrifice saved Africa.

We are used to thinking of how many vocations are lost because of egotistical parents, but perhaps we do not think enough of all the fathers and mothers who don't hesitate to give even their only child to God and mankind.

To these unknown, uncounted heroes and heroines of whom the world takes no care and of whom the world is not worthy, we bow out of profound veneration and gratitude.

Without them the legion of Apostles and Saints would never have been.

Limone on Lake Garda–Comboni's birthplace

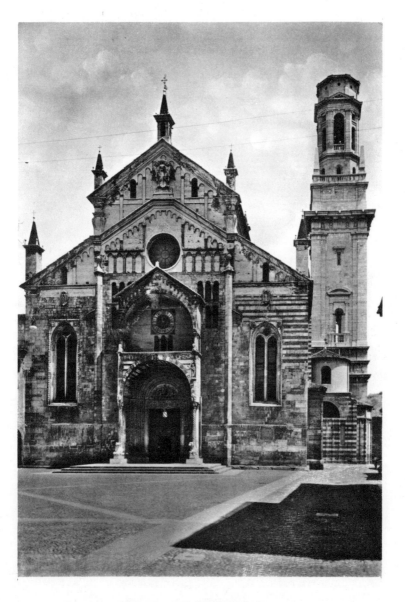

The old Cathedral of Verona,
where Comboni received his First Communion

Father Nicola Mazza

The "Morning Star"

The "hubub"—a sand storm near Khartoum, Sudan

Father Angelo Vinco—the first Missionary
on the White Nile, Sudan

One of Father Vinco's friends

2

THE IMPOSSIBLE

1857-1872

"UPSTREAM THE WHITE NILE"

"Bless, O Lord, these children with a large, full blessing. Keep them good and faithful till death.— And you, my dear ones, go now in the name of God. Never forget that the work to which you consecrated your lives belongs wholly to Him: do all and exclusively for Him. Love and respect each other, try to agree in everything. The glory of God, the sole glory of God mean and promote. Everything else is vanity."

Raising his eyes up toward heaven, inspiringly the saintly Father Mazza blessed his six chosen ones, kneeling around him. Then he embraced them and kissed them all one by one.

They sailed from Trieste on September 10, 1857. At Alexandria, Egypt, Father Beltrame, the superior of the group, and Father Oliboni got busy preparing for the crossing of the desert. Their first goal was Khartoum where the Pro-Vicar Knoblecher was waiting for them.

The others, Fathers Melotto, Dal Bosco, Comboni and Brother Zilli very willingly accepted a free trip to the Holy Land, offered by the Franciscan Fathers.

Father Daniel passed one night in the Grotto of Bethlehem where he could offer the Holy Sacrifice and he kissed almost every stone. He also passed two nights in prayer at the Holy Sepulcher where he said Mass two times. He wrote home: "Oh, how wonderful!... I was insulted by these people, but what are insults here where Jesus was crucified?..."

Back at Alexandria, the young Knight of the Dark Continent is ready for anything. His war cry echoes in his intrepid heart clearer than ever: "Africa or Death!"

After a murderous trip through the desert, our Missionaries reached Khartoum, January 8, 1858. In a couple of weeks the anxious young Missionaries were ready to continue for the interior, via the White Nile. They sailed on the mission boat, "Morning Star," which the good Pro-Vicar Knoblecher put at their disposal. It was January 21, 1858. Father Dal Bosco remained at Khartoum as Procurator.

Father Comboni in a long letter to his parents describes the fascinating trip: "The White Nile is so wide that it looks more like a lake than a river... The vegetation on both banks is very picturesque ... Swarms of birds of every size and color fly back and forth from all directions and some even come to rest on the ropes of our boat. Ibis, wild ducks, pelicans and many other big specimens often walk on the ground or stand looking up to heaven as if giving thanks for God's loving care of them. Herds of monkeys run to the river to drink and move away jumping up and down the trees, playing like mischievous youngsters. . . . Hundreds of antelopes and gazelles are grazing undisturbed: Never a shot has broken the silence of their green Eden. . . . Huge crocodiles are lying lazily on small sandy isles. . . . Enormous hippos are puffing in the water and their sinister bellowing in the evening makes our blood curl. . . . But we are used to it now and everything leads our thoughts to God. How immense and powerful He must be. . . ."

Of course the trip was not always so rosy. At times, the White Nile became an immense swamp and the heavy boat got stuck in the mud. All the crew had to get into the water and work very hard at times to get it going again. The worst incident of this kind happened near Mocada-el-Kelb. It was midnight. A most beautiful bright moon shone in the sky and on both banks of the river the savages around big bonfires were looking on the intruder boat perhaps carrying slave traders.

"Our situation is critical." writes Father Daniel. "We are stuck here in the very middle at the White Nile. On one side we have Dinka tribes famous for their cruelty. This past year they massacred the entire crew of Latiff Effendi from Khartoum. On the other side, lives the Schilluk tribe, the most powerful and ferocious of all Central Africa. And we cannot move one single inch. These savages could attack us and destroy us in no time. We have in the boat about ten guns, but missionaries prefer to be murdered a hundred times rather than defend themselves. We are sure Jesus would have done the same. Do you know what our plans are? If the Schilluks attack, we will all become their slaves and with the grace of God we will preach to them Christ crucified. Our mission will be right here.... But we have a most powerful weapon. In the Morning Star there is a very beautiful picture of the Blessed Mother. How could this our good Mother see us suffering and not come to our help? In the morning we said Mass. How wonderful to touch with our very hands and receive in our hearts the Lord of all rivers and tribes of the world. Needless to say, I pray for you, dear Mom and Dad, for my companions here and for all. A special prayer was offered for the Dinkas and Schilluks who never heard of our Divine faith...."

All the crew tried to move the boat but to no avail. Some of our men, with signs of all kinds, called on the savages for help. A few of them very cautiously came, but they asked for gifts first and, as soon as they had them, quickly disappeared. After one more day and one more night of useless efforts, they were finally on their way again.

Being completely out of meat, they stopped at Kako to buy an ox. For the occasion a tribe-chief was invited into the boat where they showed him the chapel. The savage put his hand at his mouth and yelled a prolonged "hoooo" and backed out fast. Confronted with a mirror he started to talk and laugh and jump, but when he saw that the other fellow was always doing the very same thing he ran away in despair.

Father Daniel, the youngest of the group, was always eager to know more about the customs of the different tribes. When the "Morning Star" stopped at Fandah-el-Eliab he went to see a kind of market among the Nuer. He liked to observe the most fantastic fashions of the natives. Some had their hair fixed with mud and flour falling around their head like a little tail. Others were wearing something like a periwig shaped like a helmet and all covered with little pearls. Others had their hair just straight up in the air. Some wore pieces of brass or copper on their forehead. All had from two to five ivory bracelets around their arms. Naturally, women had all that, plus! Their necks were covered with seed pearls; they wore at least a dozen bracelets and from their ears was hanging almost anything. Even their upper lip was pierced through by a sharp piece of metal or glass. Fashion indeed has its victims everywhere!

After twenty-five days on the White Nile, the Morning Star docked at the missionary station of Holy Cross, some thousand miles south of Khartoum. It was February 14, 1858. Father Joseph Lanz came to meet them, out of himself with joy. He was all alone. His companion Father Mozgan had succumbed to the terrible climate.

"We will stay here for a while", wrote Father Daniel, "so we can learn the language of the natives and explore a suitable place for our foundation. In the meantime God will manifest to us His will."

HOLY CROSS

The Morning Star continued its route towards Gondokoro, the extreme south station some seventy miles from Holy Cross.

Our young missionaries could at last settle down and start living the life in the jungle they had spoken and dreamed so much about during the long years of preparation in Verona. They were happy. Father Beltrame, the superior, wrote; "I am practicing the trade of my father who is a good carpenter. Father Oliboni is making bread. Father Melotto takes care of the laundry and Father Comboni is busy with needle and thread . . . soon we will sow some vegetables and corn . . ."

There was no word of Brother Zilli. The good brother had been attacked almost immediately by persistent fever. When, a few weeks later the Morning Star, back from Gondokoro, stopped at Holy Cross on its way to Khartoum, Brother was sent there. Meanwhile, the superior of Gondokoro had died.

The rainy season was approaching and with it the urgent need to build new huts and cover the roofs very carefully with much straw. The natives were friendly and some even offered to help.

With Father Lanz they planned and built a little church. Its frame was of ebony filled in with adobe bricks. The Africans were amazed at the great things that the white man could do.

"We say Mass here," wrote Father Comboni, "and we are happier than if we were in the big cathedrals of Europe. The chiefs come with their people even from far away and how they behave in church!"

Together with material work went the daily study of the language of the natives. Their results in this field sound like a prodigy. In only a month they had prepared a dictionary of some three thousand words, with grammar, dialogues and familiar expressions and a little catechism. The magic of these terrific activities and results, however, was soon coming to an end. Again man's plans proved not to be God's plans. On March 19, Father Oliboni unexpectedly became very ill and in two hours he was critical. Of his companions in deep consternation, he calmly and serenely asked for the last sacraments and tried to console them. On March 26 he was dead. The remaining three felt lost. Their "saint" was not with them any more. The interior life of Oliboni was of a degree that only saints ever reached. His austerity with himself was beyond imitation. His sweetness proverbial. Lying on a blanket on the dirt floor of his hut and looking at his companions who were crying like children, he had had the inspiration of saying to them, like his last will: "My dear Brothers, I am dying and I am glad because God wants it so. Please don't get discouraged. Never give up ... even ... yes, even if only one will be left. I am positive God wants this African mission and the conversion of the Africans. I die with this absolute certainty. ..."

He was another generous one dying in Africa for Africa.

Daniel Comboni could only answer for himself. Kneeling at Oliboni's side, his face in his hands, he renewed, without conditions or reservations, his solemn oath to go on at any price, till the very last breath. Father Marani had assured him of his vocation so there could be no doubt: either Africa or death! His war cry was receiving its first baptism of blood. Whether saintly Oliboni was conscious of making a prophecy we will never know. The fact is that actually only one was going to be left and this was the youngest of the group, Daniel Comboni.

GOING UP TO CALVARY

Father Beltrame made the coffin and dear Oliboni was buried close to Father Mozgan. On the little wooden cross was inscribed: "I am the Resurrection and the Life."

The end of March was the beginning of the rainy season and with it the most frightening storms ever seen. The roar of the lion and the bellowing of hundreds of beasts in the surrounding forest added to the situation to make it a real "inferno". Suddenly the fields and the trees turned green. The wild animals migrated and, whereas before they used to pass the Mission yard at night to reach the river, now they hung around the huts of the Missionaries who often had the unpleasant company of elephants, buffaloes, giraffes and now and then the visit of the leopard and the lion.

The moisture became unbearable. Everything inside the huts was covered with thick mold. Clothes, papers, everything reeked with a terrible stench. Termites were everywhere. Thousands of mosquitoes tormented our Missionaries day and night. Snakes and big scorpions joined in every once in a while. And naturally with it all the unfriendly visit of "sister malaria," the treacherous intermittent fever against which they had practically nothing to fight with.

Father Daniel wrote: "This fever has a special liking for me. From April 6 to August 15 it was almost always my inseparable companion. Once I had it very very high for eleven straight days."

The real Africa little by little was opening itself before our courageous young men from Verona, like a huge volume of the most fantastic novel. All the indescribable miseries of a people deeply buried in barbarity were coming to their attention. And on top of it all, and worst of all, slavery practiced on a very large scale by the white man with the help of local chiefs and renegades. "Poor, poor Africa bleeding frightfully from all its pores!" was the sad comment of Father Daniel. The slave traders had preceded the missionaries. The thirst for gold proved again to be more effective than love.

On November 13, the first steam-boat ever seen on the White Nile cast anchor at Holy Cross. It was Mr. Lafargue with lots of mail from Khartoum and Europe. What a relief to receive news from the loved ones after ten months of complete isolation! But unfortunately it was only a long, long necrology. Pro-Prefect Knoblecher had died April 13; three days later Father Gosner, Superior of Khartoum had died; their Brother Zilli had died June 11. Father Kirchner, temporary head of the African Mission had gone to Rome for consultation. Their companion Father Dal Bosco, all alone at Khartoum, was very

weak from repeated attacks of fever. A personal
letter to Father Comboni told him of the death of his
beloved mother on June 14.

He wrote immediately to his father and also
begged some of his fellow Priests at Verona to,
"please, see him and console him." And to Father
Bricolo: "How terrible to have my father all alone!
But I am sure this is for the best. May God be
blessed!"

After all this disastrous news the four Missionaries from Verona got together and, in the end, the
idea of abandoning Holy Cross prevailed. The main
reasons were three: It was an extremely unhealthy
place; it was too close to camps of slave traders who
were infesting the region with their unmentionable
depravities; Father Dal Bosco was all alone and perhaps still very sick. They would go back to him and
there wait for instructions. A boat had come from
Khartoum for them so they had to say good-bye. A
sad evening! After having wept over the tomb of
dearest Oliboni, they warmly embraced Father Lanz
and his companions who were staying till a defininte
decision from the Pro-Vicar was taken. How hard to
leave the brave companions of such dark days! It
was January 15, 1859.

While going back to Khartoum, Fathers Beltrame and Melotto tried to look around for a suitable
place for a new Mission in the possible future, while

Father Daniel was obliged to lie in the boat all during the long trip, crushed by the intermittent fevers. They landed at Khartoum, April 4, 1859.

Father Melotto never felt so good all during his stay in Africa. Suddenly, May 24, a violent attack of fever obliged him to take to bed. By May 28 he was dead. Like Father Oliboni, before dying he insisted on and begged his confreres not to give up the idea of Central Africa. His first name was Angelo and they say he really died an angelic death with his handsome face radiating a mysterious charm. His passing away was always remembered as a scene of heaven.

Since there seemed no way to kill the fever that was tormenting Father Daniel, he was obliged, by Fathers Beltrame and Dal Bosco, to leave for home. He gave in only to an explicit command and cried like a child, August 1859.

At the end of the same year he was at Verona, then at Limone. To the good people of Limone he looked literally destroyed, a walking ghost. One Sunday afternoon the Pastor having to answer a sick call, Father Daniel took his place in the explanation of the Catechism to the adults in church, but not even those in the front pews could hear him. The good people, who remembered the great orator he used to be, were all in tears as they repeated to each other: "Oh, how right his mother was in saying that he was going to die down there. He is not dead yet, but he certainly doesn't have long to live." And they competed with one another in bringing him all kinds of foods and fruits and exquisite wines. How many tried to make him change his mind about Central Africa. But he knew now too much about it. The tombs of his brothers along the White Nile were calling him desperately. Oh never, never could he change his mind. He was "ready to die a thousand deaths for those wretched, unforgettable tribes." Yes, unconditionally "Africa or Death!"

Meanwhile, the poor beloved Mission was agonizing.

When he felt better Father Daniel was back in Verona, with dear Father Mazza who put him in charge of the few little Africans that were getting an education at St. Charles.

At the end of 1860, Father Mazza was offered some more of these poor children, ex-slaves, but he had to go as far as Aden in Saudi Arabia to get them. Father Daniel was happy to take his place. With a special blessing from Pope Pius IX and papers from almost all the governments of Europe, he crossed the Red Sea and came back to Verona with the children after one of the most fabulous trips. Among other things he was thrown in jail at Alexandria, Egypt. But his indomitable courage and blind trust in Divine Providence had to triumph.

He was ready to return to Africa and join Fathers Beltrame and Dal Bosco in the station of Shellal, when Father Mazza received a message from the new Pro-Prefect Kirchner: "The condition of the Mission of Central Africa is desperate. I feel obliged in conscience to call in a Religious Order or to abandon everything. We are killing Missionaries and wasting money for nothing." Kirchner himself came to Rome and, after laborious negotiations, the Superior General of the Franciscans agreed to take over in Central Africa.

This sounded like a sentence of death for Father Comboni and his beloved Father Mazza. But saints never give up. Some of the African children could not stand the climate of Verona, so Father Mazza, as he had done before, sent Father Comboni to Naples with them, to Father Ludovico, O.F.M., who was also taking care of African children freed from slavery. But Father Mazza was careful to tell Comboni to go to Rome, on the way back from Naples, and see the Prefect of Propaganda Fide about Central Africa. This stay of Comboni's in Rome was most evidently planned by God's Providence. It gave him the chance to know very well several Cardinals and especially Cardinal Barnabo, Prefect of Propaganda. It gave him the opportunity to help and get acquainted with many Societies of Sisters, particularly the Sisters of Saint Joseph. He became intimate with Pope Pius IX. He even became a close friend of some noble families and princes of Rome. All these friends Daniel would need very soon.

Meanwhile, at the end of 1861, the Franciscans were in Khartoum: Father Reinthaler, Pro-Prefect, with six other Fathers and twenty-eight Lay-Brothers. But many of the heroic Missionaries died even before having started any work. Pro-Prefect Reinthaler was among them: April 1862. About this time Father Mazza suspended indefinitely his plans for Central Africa.

The Franciscans promptly sent another expedition of twenty-three more Missionaries. But these met with the same fate. The survivors decided to abandon Central Africa altogether. It was clear now that the unfortunate Mission was a lost cause. The immense territory stretching from Egypt to the great lakes at the Equator was attached, for the time being, to the Vicariate Apostolic of Egypt. 1864.

In sixteen years some forty-four Missionaries had died along the White Nile. Central Africa was just impossible!

THE PLAN

Napoleon once said, they claim, that the word "impossible" could be found only in the vocabulary of idiots. Unfortunately, history has proved either his statement wrong or that he too was, after all, one of those fools he was talking about.

Any human cause can be subject to failure, the Napoleonic cause included. Only God's cause cannot fail in the end. Only for God the word "impossible" does not exist. Convinced of this elementary truth, the young missionary Daniel Comboni stops in spirit at the threshold of the "forbidden" dark continent, admits the defeat of the initial battles, but is profoundly convinced that only the last battle makes one win or lose a war. To retreat in order to reorganize, to study a new strategy: yes! To surrender? Never! "Africa or Death".

Eighteen hundred sixty-two and sixty-three were two years of intense traveling for Father Daniel. He journeyed all through Italy, France, Germany, Austria, Switzerland to see other institutions for foreign missions and to make as many friends as possible for the financial needs of Central Africa.

He stopped in all the convents he could to solicit prayers and sacrifices. Meanwhile, he himself was desperately begging God and His Mother for light and guidance. Back in Verona he felt urged to leave immediately for Rome where great celebrations were underway for the beatification of Margaret Alacoque, the humble confidante of the Sacred Heart.

On September 15, the first day of the triduum in honor of the new Beata, Father Daniel was praying hard at the tomb of Saint Peter. Suddenly an inspiration struck him. Out of all the experiences and consultations of years, a definite central idea took form in his mind and became clearer and clearer. He ran to his room and in sixty almost consecutive hours he put in writing his famous "Plan for the Salvation of Africa".

"I think it comes from God," he informed Father Mazza. "I wrote it during the triduum, and Cardinal Barnabo finished reading it the very day of the Beatification of Margaret Mary."

It was the first blessing of the new Beata on the young missionary who will later found and develop all his works for Africa at the warmth of the devotion of the Sacred Heart of Jesus.

The central idea of his inspired Plan is "The conversion of Africa by Africa." This amazing conviction of Father Daniel concerning an African clergy closely assisted by native lay apostles calls to our mind the admirable encyclicals written in our times by Pope Benedict XV, Pius XI, Pius XII, John XXIII on this very same subject. Comboni goes as far as suggesting the foundation of at least four African universities situated intelligently in four important African centers. How clear the desperate need for future leaders must have been in the mind of this "great leader!" Naturally only God knows the future but in the meantime we can't help thinking that if Comboni's Plan had somehow been carried out, perhaps we wouldn't have had the unpleasant happenings all over Africa in 1961, which culminated in the tragedy of Belgian Congo, whose sad consequences will be felt for many years to come.

Father Daniel did not aspire to any personal leadership in this great endeavor, but suggested instead the co-ordination of all forces, old and new, under the supreme command of Propaganda Fide. All united for victory and the salvation of the entire African Continent

Cardinal Barnabo liked the Plan as a whole. So did other Cardinals and Bishops. Pope Pius IX received Father Daniel in private audience three times. Through Cardinal Barnabo the Holy Father had him called again October 28. This time they talked together about the Plan in the Holy Father's bedroom. The paternal ways of Pope Pius IX, so humble and cordial, Father Daniel would never forget. At the end, the Pope concluded, "I am so glad you think of Africa. Now go to Paris, show your Plan to the Society of the Propagation of the Faith there. Then according to the help you will get, Cardinal Barnabo will write a circular letter to all the

Vicars and Prefects Apostolic of Africa and I will sign the decree of approval. I charge you to study the way to associate the Plan with the other institutions and societies. I give you my blessing. Keep working as a good soldier of Christ for Africa."

In one of these audiences, most probably the last one, the sweet Pius IX found himself against the wall. There was nothing malicious about it—it was just that Father Daniel proved to be a very convinced and a very convincing orator for Africa. No wonder the angelic Pope baptized him "My African."

THE LAST BLOW

Father Daniel made arrangements to leave immediately for France according to the order of the Holy Father. After stopping at Verona to report to Father Mazza, he passed from Bressanone to see his good friend, Canon Mitterrutzner, and to show him his Plan. Finally, he left for France, stopping first at Turin. In this beautiful city he was guest of St. John Bosco, whose boys he inflamed for Africa. In Turin he had his Plan printed in all the European languages and mailed it ahead of him to all the different places he was planning to go. Here he also had the pleasure of meeting the great Catholic writer Alessandro Manzoni.

Through the Alps, via St. Bernard, he arrived in Lyons, France, where one of the central councils for the Propagation of the Faith was, the other being in Paris. His stay in Lyons was very short. His Plan meeting with some obstacles here, he decided to answer the call of Bishop Massaia, the Vicar Apostolic of the Gallas, Ethopia, who was inviting him to Paris.

January 11, 1865. It was the first time the two great Apostles of Africa met. They understood each other immediately and from that day forward their most intimate friendship never failed. The saintly

Bishop wrote to Propaganda Fide on February 10, 1865: "I am so edified by this young priest, and his zeal for the conversion of Africa is a good lesson God gives me from which I will try to get the most . . . I dedicated myself to the conversion of the Gallas and I thought I did something, but here I find a heart much larger that carries the weight of all Africa and would convert it all . . . How admirable! . . . "

The Apostle of the Gallas was anxious to present Comboni to the most influential persons of Paris, both clergy and laity. They even met the empress Eugenia Napoleon. With his exquisite way of dealing with people, and his terrific eloquence, Father Daniel was always stealing the show to the immense delight of Bishop Massaia who wrote of him: "God enriched this young man with so much virtue and zeal and with so many gifts of nature that he is bound to become a model of missionaries. Endowed with a superior energy and iron will, he could dare anything. Much more learned than myself, and gifted with a unique eloquence, he is easily winning the esteem and love of all."

The central council for the Propagation of the Faith of Paris, with many other societies, promised him their wholehearted support. Father Daniel wrote to Father Bricolo, the rector of Saint Charles, under Father Mazza: "Everything is fine up here. Very good financially. The difficult thing is to get the religious orders together for the foundations according to the will of the Holy Father. . . . Lots of interest for Africa here in France. With the help of holy grace, I will always try to work under the inspiration of God and to co-operate with Him for the salvation of the poor Africans."

From Paris he went to Cologne, Germany, where the "Society for the Little Africans" promised its full financial support. Then called by Cardinal Wiseman concerning his Plan for Africa, he passed on to London. Unfortunately, the great Cardinal had died in the meantime. From London, back to Paris. From Paris to Amiens, where the Bishop was planning an institution for African Slaves. From Amiens to Orleans, where he was the guest of famous Bishop Dupanloup. Then to Spain and back to Paris, where bad news was waiting for him. He was officially expelled from the institute of Father Mazza! Diabolical tongues had succeeded in fooling the saintly old man.

The move came so unexpectedly that Comboni was "shocked" and Massaia "petrified" as they both confessed later. The saintly Bishop sent at once a desperate imploring note to Father Mazza in Latin on the back of a photograph of himself and Comboni. Father Daniel immediately wrote a long letter ending with: "No, No. I cannot live away from the heart of my Father. . . . If you chase me out of the door, I will come back through the window. . . . Scold me, punish me, beat me up, but don't send me away. I want to be in your heart and till death your most loving son. Will see you very soon, very, very soon."

A few days later he was in Verona at the feet of his Father. "Father, I don't even ask why you expelled me from the institute, but if you really believe what they told you, please write here: I, Father Mazza, declare that Daniel Comboni for twenty-three years attached to my institute does not belong to it any more." The saintly old priest after a few seconds fell upon Father Daniel's neck and kissed him: "You are my son!" And knowing from a letter Bishop Massaia had written to him, that his Daniel was going to Rome, Father Mazza asked him about it. The Nuncio of Paris, Archbishop Chigi and Bishop Massaia himself were sending him to see the Holy Father and Cardinal Antonelli for very important and pressing matters.

"I think I have something very important, too, all for you," interrupted Father Mazza. "Please, wait. Don't leave right away." After a brief consultation with Father Beltrame, the old man gave to his beloved son the greatest gift of all: a letter for Cardinal Barnabo in which he was asking for a mission in Central Africa. How good God was to his faithful servant. Not only was He giving him back the love of his dear Father, but He had him active again in the realization of his Plan.

Out of himself with joy, Father Daniel left for Rome. Cardinal Barnabo was pleased at the request of Father Mazza, but he sent Father Comboni to talk to the general of the Franciscans who, at least nominally, were still in charge of the Vicariate of Central Africa.

In the meantime, Father Daniel was notified of the death of Father Mazza on August 2, 1865. This was a totally unexpected blow. He wrote later: "I left Verona never to see again here below the one who gave me a second life and who for twenty-three years had been a most loving Father, teacher, and guide. His ardent zeal burned for Africa to the end."

The general of the Franciscans delegated Father Ludovico of Naples, an old friend of Comboni, to decide the matter. Since Father Ludovico had already asked for himself the little station of Shellal, Cardinal Barnabo advised both to go to Africa in order to see on the spot what was the best thing to do.

The trip was disastrous. The ship broke in two and they considered it a miracle to have their lives saved. From Shellal, Father Ludovico had to hurry back because the cholera morbus had broken out in his foundations in Naples. In March, Father Comboni was back in Rome for his report.

One month later the successor of Father Mazza definitely withdrew his institute from any work in Africa. Father Ludovico also could not co-operate any longer since the plague had killed almost all his African children.

That evening to Father Comboni, sitting with face in his hands, came back as clear as in a picture the White Nile, the wild forest at Holy Cross and that far distant March 28, 1858, with dear Father Francis Oliboni dying on the dirt floor of his hut: "If only one should be left . . . let him never doubt . . . never give up . . ."

"No, never . . . Africa or Death."

ALL ALONE

The darker the night, the brighter the stars shine in the sky. How identically true for Comboni's vocation.

Many bishops and particularly lay people were all in favor of the Plan for the Salvation of Africa, but religious orders looked at it rather coldly. His own institute was out of the race forever. What next? All the material help possible was useless without element number one: missionaries. Should he give up?

"I could have a great career," he wrote, "if I wanted to, though unworthy, but what about Africa? Shall I let all those millions of souls be lost? No, no, we must try again, only trusting in the One who loves all men and wants them all safe." And to Father Bricolo: "I will have plenty to suffer from some who are doing their best to oppose my efforts, but I also have high hopes, great supports and all confidence in God. Of one thing I am particularly positive: that the Plan is the clear will of God. . . . Equally certain it is that God has given me a boundless confidence in Him, that I will never give up and that for Central Africa a new era will begin soon."

And begin he did all over again, all alone. Early in 1867 he had an appointment with his

bishop of Verona, Louis Canossa, later a cardinal.
He was well known by him since 1849. The great
Bishop agreed to take under his protection the two
foundations Father Daniel was going to make for
missionary priests and missionary sisters. Back from
Rome he rented a house for future priests and a
good widow gave him her house for the sisters.
When reporting to his Bishop about this first step
he also asked for the man to put in charge of the
two institutions, while he would continue to be the
professional beggar for Africa throughout Europe.
The man proposed by Comboni was Father Alexander Dal Bosco, one of his conpanions of the first
expedition to Central Africa, in 1857.

The saintly man obeyed the wish of his Bishop
though sincerely protesting to be unfit for such a
difficult assignment. But he was most happy to start
working again for Africa with his beloved Father
Daniel.

To assure a steady flow of funds for his works,
Comboni created the Association of the Good Shepherd for which Bishop Canossa provided the proper
canonical approval with an inspired comment on
the Plan for the Salvation of Africa. On June 1, 1867,
the pious prelate also gave an indulgence to the
ejaculation "Queen of Africa, pray for us."

The very solemn celebrations in Rome for the
18th Centenary of the martyrdom of the Prince of
the Apostles took Father Daniel to Rome with his

Bishop. Here he had the third edition of his Plan printed for all the members of the hierarchy and illustrious visitors from all over the world.

Cardinal Barnabo gave his temporary approval to the institutions of Verona and Pius IX granted six plenary indulgences to the Association of the Good Shepherd.

While Comboni was taking care of the spreading of the Association beyond the Alps, Bishop Canossa in a circular letter in Latin was inviting all the Bishops of Italy to establish it in their dioceses.

The second step to take, according to the Plan, was on the African shores. Pope Pius IX suggested Cairo, so Father Daniel immediately discarded his other plans and got busy to get ready for the Cairo foundations. He did not have personnel of his own yet, but Divine Providence came to his rescue with Mother Emilie Julien, superior of the Sisters of the Apparition of St. Joseph, who assigned three Sisters for Cairo. At the same time three Camillian Fathers asked their superiors for permission to join Comboni in his expedition to Africa. Again God had not failed the boundless confidence of his missionary.

At the end of November Comboni had ready in Marseilles three Fathers, three Sisters and sixteen African girls educated in Europe. On November 29 they all sailed for Cairo. While in Marseilles Father Daniel was again able to see and encourage in her vocation, Mother Marie Deluil Martiny, the foundress of the Daughters of the Sacred Heart and the apostle of the Guard of Honor of the Heart of Jesus. Father Daniel with his usual frankness had told this privileged soul: "You are unworthy of it all, but you have to admit God gave you the secret of this heavenly endeavor." She would never forget that.

As soon as they arrived in Cairo, Comboni provided two separate buildings, one for the boys and the other for the girls. He dedicated the first to the Heart of Jesus, the other to the Immaculate Heart of Mary. Poor slaves or ex-slaves, many in the most pitiable condition, started to flock in. With material relief they also received some schooling and religious instruction. Many were baptized and some became fervent lay apostles. Soon a regular school and trade school were added to the infirmary. For his collaborators as well as for the inmates, Father Comboni laid down very practical rules which reveal how well prepared he was for this task and how wisely he was able to coordinate his many European experiences to this end.

After seven months he was back in Europe to continue his begging job. He wrote to his Bishop: "I have tongue to ask, pen to write, courage to accept refusals. . . ." On July 16, 1868, he landed at Marseilles and on the 23 he was at Our Lady of LaSalette. There he met with his friend Mr. Girard, with Bishop Millos, Vicar Apostolic of Galdea, and, two days later, with Bishop Salzano of Naples.

On July 26 in the great Basilica after the pontifical Mass of Bishop Salzano, Bishop Millos consecrated his vicariate to the Blessed Mother, followed by Comboni who between the two Bishops read his act of Consecration of Central Africa to the Mother of God. On the evening of the same day Comboni delivered the closing sermon. In it the tremendous lover of Mary and of Africa reached such desperate accents that all present in the Basilica were in tears. And in closing he thus addressed the Blessed Mother: "Before leaving, O my Mother, I will tell you another word of anguish. I know I will pierce your heart, but you have wept on this mountain over the sorrows of your people, and the Africans are your people also. Think, O Mother, that the hundreds of millions of Africans I offered you this morning are all condemned to Hell . . . all will be lost if you don't help them. Dearest Mother, please don't permit that. Yes, think that you have there a hundreds of millions of Africans who stretch their arms towards you weeping and imploring: "Queen of Africa, save us! We will all go to Hell if you don't come to our rescue."

When he came down from the pulpit the superior of LaSalette embraced him saying: "The Holy Virgin must answer your prayer. We will keep reminding her. . . ."

The following day all were asking for the Missionary of Africa and he did receive generous donations for his institutions. He left the same day for Grenoble, where he preached again. Then he reached Lyons and, from there, Paris.

Meanwhile, a new idea was maturing in his mind. Things were rolling now in France; why not establish here also the Association of the Good Shepherd and later, when times were ripe, a seminary for Central Africa? The famous Augustus Nicolas spoke in favor of the ideas at the General Council for the Propagation of the Faith. Mr. Baudon, General President of the St. Vincent De Paul societies, promised Comboni fifty thousand francs annually. Others joined the committee with Baron Havelt, French minister for foreign affairs, Count Courcelles, ex-ambassador to Rome, Counts Merode and Segure, Monsignor Valette of Notre Dame and Monsignor Reineval of La Madeleine, Edmund Lefont, president of St. Peter's Society.

The paper "Apostolat" of Paris was ready to publish the decree for the erection of the Association of the Good Shepherd, but naturally Comboni wanted to ask his own Bishop of Verona first. Then out of the blue sky came the mysterious blow. Canossa thought it prudent not to start the Association of the Good Shepherd in France at all and to suspend it in Italy as well because it was perhaps against the wishes of Cardinal Barnabo. So he thought.

This advice is hard to understand when we know that Pius IX himself, on July 15, 1867, had signed the decree of approval of the Association of the Good Shepherd with the granting of six plenary indulgences. Or was it Divine Providence that had decreed to have the Comboni institutions only around Verona for a long time to come? Or was it just another one of those crosses Comboni was always praying for? Whatever it was, the fact is that Comboni agreed to leave at once, according to Bishop Canossa's advice, although "terribly embarrassed before his noble friends."

This is sound heroism, we have to admit. This young man of a superior intelligence, so quick in grasping the central point of the most intricate problems, so capable that in a foreign country and speaking a foreign language he could conquer for his cause—the cause of Africa—the best minds of the time; this young priest who at thirty-seven had already left his country for Africa four times and travelled all through Europe; who was a dear friend of the Holy Father, Cardinals, Bishops, and heads of governments; this young missionary was certainly proving beyond a doubt that, as of now, he had reached a superb control of his naturally impetuous character and most certainly was travelling swiftly towards heroic sanctity.

And still the "Verona order" was just the beginning of sorrows. In fact, at this time Comboni was notified that the imprudence of one of his missionaries had almost ruined everything in Cairo. A few days later, on December 13, a telegram from

Limone announced that his father was critically sick. On December 14, a telegram from Verona announced that "Father Dal Bosco was not going to live through the day." On December 15, a second telegram came from Verona with the sad news of Dal Bosco's death.

One of Comboni's biographers likens him, at this particular time of his life, to Job of old and indeed how rightly so.

We would think that "now" he must at last give in and forget about Africa. But of course we are wrong. For on December 20, he is writing to his Bishop: "In my immense sorrow for the death of our beloved Dal Bosco what comforts me is that Jesus sends us crosses. . . . All my confidence is in God and in the Queen of Africa . . . the Hearts of Jesus and Mary will triumph. . . ."

At this turning point his war cry "Africa or Death" really tunes up to the "superhuman."

MURDER

Paris, December 22, 1868. Father Comboni is packing in a hurry for Verona. His good host, Baron Havelt, is with him. Around ten P.M. the doorbell rings. A distinguished gentleman asks for the Missionary from Africa. When Comboni is introduced to him the stranger says bluntly: "Father, a man is dying and he wants only you."

Comboni, rather used to such calls in Paris does not lose a second and after having reminded the good Baron not to stay up waiting for him he is outdoors. A beautiful landau is parked close by. He gets in and the two horses start trotting fast. One gentleman is sitting at his side and two others in front of him. Nobody talks. The intelligent missionary immediately realizes that there is something mysterious and sinister about this night adventure he put himself into without much thinking. In fact, not before long the one sitting at his side says coldly: "I have to blindfold you."

"What? Is this not a sick call?"

"Yes, it is. And yet I have to blindfold you."

"You will not blindfold me! . . ." But Comboni hardly has time to jump to his feet that the two in front are at his chest, one with a knife and the other with a pistol.

97

Well, there wasn't much else to do, so he let them blindfold him. Nobody ever said a word anymore. The landau kept going and going for about two hours. Comboni really thought that he was taking a trip to eternity; but actually he was not, for the horses stopped at last.

"We have to get off now," said one. "Give me your hand and watch your step." Comboni is taken inside a house and again around they go, through rooms and corridors. Finally, he is told to sit down and his eyes are uncovered. The sitting room is beautifully decorated and flooded with lights.

"In there is the sick person, Reverend!" and one of the rascals almost pushed Father Daniel into an adjacent room where hanging on the knob of the door he added: "You have one hour of time." Then he banged the door and hurried away. "Thanks," said Father Daniel who thought that this was the end.

"Please, sit down, Father, make yourself comfortable. I am the sick man you came to help to die." The gentleman who was speaking looked anything but sick. Father Daniel thought of another dirty trick: "Yes," he answered, "I see you people have fooled me. But do you think you will be able to fool God also?"

"No, Father, no, and this is why I called on you. You see, I'm not sick at all and yet one hour of life is all I have left. I will tell you briefly. I am a

Freemason and I am now a prisoner of the very sect to which I belonged and served for twenty-eight years. My courage and determination in the most hazardous crimes pushed me up step by step to the top. I am a '33rd degree Mason.' Days ago I was assigned to the killing of a very well-known and esteemed prelate. [1] I refused. I knew what my refusal meant, but, I don't know myself why I did refuse and I'm glad I did. In one hour from now they will drag me into the fatal room and with a big fork they will open my two jugular veins at the collar bone. That way the wound will hardly be noticed. It is our way of getting rid of our 'friends'. I did it many times to others and God in His infinite mercy makes me go the very same way. They will throw my corpse in the Seine River. You might be able to see it exposed later in the public mortuary in Paris."

"What you are saying might be true," observed Father Daniel still rather skeptical, "but how do you explain the fact that these people took the trouble to call a priest for you, when all know that they never allow one to their dying affiliates?"

"I was accepted in the secret sect for my very influential position in society with the explicit understanding to have a priest before my death. The condition was accepted and it is all in the interest of the sect to keep promises made to its candidates."

[1] These are the "old" freemasons of the "old" country, we have to remember.

"All right, but why call on an unknown foreigner like me?"

"Yes, you are a foreigner, but by all means not unknown to the Freemasons of Paris. They know you better than you think. They know how good you are in lost cases like mine. Your last conversion made among our ranks is the one of Mr. X . . ." and he mentioned the name of a young man Comboni did receive into the Church not long before, who was a member of the sect, with his entire family, father, mother, and four sisters, all paid well to spread the sect around Paris. "Yes, this is the last of many. Besides, the fact that you are a foreigner and above all a missionary is just what they want. You are here today and gone tomorrow. If you should stay around too long you could perhaps find out this place and that is what they don't want. Dear Father, I am so grateful that you came for me also. I made all my studies in schools run by the Jesuits. Deep in my heart I am and always have been a Catholic. Of course, I have to admit that this is a grace of God Almighty. I know that someone is praying and suffering for me. I am sure of two at least: my wife, a very religious woman—she lives in Charle-Roy—and my daughter, here in Paris. She is a nun. But time is running out, please Father, would you hear my confession?"

The wonderful dispositions of the penitent moved Father Daniel to tears. How visible was the infinite mercy of God!

The hour had passed. Abruptly the door opened and the three rascals moved in resolutely. Father Daniel asked for half an hour more, but to no avail. The convict joined him entreating them with insistence. Finally, "Twenty minutes more," said one, "and that will be it!" And out they went banging the door.

The penitent asked Father to go to console his wife and his daughter, to beg for their forgiveness and to tell them how he was glad to die to repair in part for his crimes. He was sure now to see them in heaven.

Father Daniel took from his pocket a small notebook asking him to write for them a few words of consolation and his last farewell. The remaining minutes were passed in prayer. When the door opened again the three grabbed their victim who had only time to cry, "Father, pray for me. May God reward you."

Comboni fell on his knees in ardent prayer. The excited steps on the wooden floor soon subsided at a distance. "O Lord, he did so many wrong things, but he is sorry and You are good!"

Then the dreadful silence was broken again by fast steps coming closer and closer. When the three opened the door he saw on their hands stains of blood. They took him into a luxurious dining room where apparently a big banquet was being served. Father Daniel always considered it a miracle of the Blessed Mother that he got out unscathed from that hell. The good Brothers Mason were really celebrating and they took care to have with them some lost women, members of the sect, with the precise purpose of ruining the Apostle of Africa. At one point things got so rough that the missionary started to use his powerful fists. Those hypocrites pretended to be scandalized for what they termed impolite manners. "With devils like you I can add also kicks!" he said most resolutely. "Let's get out of here. My job is finished: take me home!"

"We will, but have your breakfast first."

"I am too tired and I am not hungry!" How could he trust those murderers? After having gotten rid of their victim they might like to get rid of the witness as well. So at their insistence he cut short: "It is past midnight and I have to say Mass. You know I must be fasting for that. Let's go!"

"Yes, we go now" said one, and coming very very close and almost thrusting his red, hellish eyes into the eyes of the missionary, he added, "Sir, you don't know a thing of all you saw here tonight; is that clear? Don't you forget that our dagger could reach you even in the very heart of Africa!" Then they blindfolded him again; again the long walking through rooms and corridors; the cold air of the night and again the long, long trotting through the darkness. Then the landau stopped, they took him off; a short walk; and a voice, "Sit down!" After a few seconds a cold frightening silence.

"And this is the end," thought Father Daniel waiting for a shot or for the promised dagger. But nothing happened and that dark silence was getting unbearable. He decided to break it, cost what it may. "What time is it?" he asked. No answer. He asked again a second, and a third time, but still no answer. "Can I take this thing off of my eyes?" No answer. So he did. The thickest darkness he ever remembered was surrounding him. He had some matches but they didn't help much. Finally, he realized he was in a garden. He knocked at a house close by but no answer. Gropingly, he at last found the gate and was out on the road.

Looking around he saw a light far away in the night. He got there as fast as he could and knocked at the door. Two surprised farmers let him in.

"Good people, answering a sick call, I got lost. Is Paris close by?"

Paris? It is three hours from here! We have to go there with our milk and vegetables. We can take you to the highway and from there by coach you can reach the Capitol.

By morning Father Daniel was back in Paris. Baron Havelt and his family were really worried and were glad to see him. After all those emotions he had to take two days rest. Then the first thing he did was to hurry to see the daughter of his convert, who belonged to the Society of the Dames of the Sacred Heart. She talked first, asking prayers for the conversion of her father. Father Daniel briefly and tactfully narrated the whole story, giving her at the end her father's note. The young religious, filled with immense joy, fell on her knees in tears. "O Father," she said. "How grateful I am. You have to know that I did offer my life to God for your beloved Africa!"

How unsearchable and unspeakable are the plans of God!

On Christmas day the paper announced that a few unidentified corpses taken from the river Seine were lying in the public mortuary. Father Comboni could easily recognize his friend from a medal he had given him and from the two big holes at the collar bone.

Men were failing him, threatening to nullify his efforts for the conversion of Africa, but God was giving him another sign of His approval together with consolations all of His own.

CARDINAL BARNABO

At the end of December, Comboni reached Limone where he thanked the Mediatrix for the speedy recovery of his dear father. He was soon back in Verona where for the first time he felt strained and uncomfortable. His seminary was practically destroyed, the Association of the Good Shepherd suspended, and still some "storm" in the air. Like the prophet he too had only ruins to weep over, but unlike the prophet he preferred to keep going instead, waiting for the time chosen by Divine Providence. No complaints, no condemnations of anyone for anything.

The eternal beggar soon left for Austria and Germany to get donations for his African children in Cairo. He had been away from them for about seven months which seemed an eternity. Finally, February 20, 1869, he sailed from Marseilles with a priest, a brother, two sisters, and an African lady, trained as a teacher. The generous donations he had collected enabled him to provide his children with the furniture they so badly needed, together with a dispensary. The good old Father Peter Taggia, O.F.M., pastor of "Old Cairo," wrote at this time to Bishop Canossa: "These institutions are doing wonders in such a short time. Not only do they assist and baptize many dying adults and children, but they also make so many converts, more than myself in so many years. The grace of God is visibly on them. Indeed, I rejoice and am so happy for this."

Bishop Meurin, S.J., Vicar Apostolic of Bombay, on his way back to Europe, had a chance to see what Comboni was doing in Cairo, and he was so well impressed that he promised to do anything he could to help him. And he kept his promise. At his first opportunity, he pleaded the cause of Comboni before the Council of the Propagation of the Faith in Lyons. Only then did the Council turn and remain in favor of him. At Cologne, the great Bishop refused any donations for himself, insisting that everything be accepted in favor of Comboni. In comparison, my mission is a bed of roses. I know Comboni: his Plan for Africa is both practical and inspiring. . . . Yes, Cologne should be proud to help a mission whose founder will be called the 'Saint Francis Xavier of Central Africa.' "

Such are witnesses free from selfishness and petty personal interests. As for himself, Comboni confessed to be: "The most useless servant on earth; not worthy to kiss the feet of his companions."

During this same year, 1869, the Sacred Congregation of Propaganda officially requested the Apostolic Delegate of Egypt, Bishop Ciurcia, for a detailed report on the work of Comboni thus far. In August, the Apostolic Delegate was able to send to Rome a most satisfactory and complete account.

Answering the strongest doubt advanced by Cardinal Barnabo concerning Comboni's ability to finance his institutions, Bishop Ciurcia stated emphatically: "It is true that his main source is only Divine Providence, but facts prove that his confidence is not in vain."

Facts—these are what Rome only asks for and believes in. And facts were given. Cardinal Barnabo was satisfied and his doubts dispelled, but it took five long years to arrive at this happy conclusion.

When on September 18, 1864, Comboni presented his Plan for the Salvation of Africa, the Cardinal showed general approval of the idea, but soon after, on September 28, 1864, he wrote to Bishop Canossa of Verona asking for information about Comboni, especially concerning his ideas in politics (it was the time of patriotic movements against the many local princes, the Pope included, for a united Italy) and his life as a priest. Bishop Canossa assured the Cardinal of the most sincere devotion of Comboni to the Holy See and expressed approval for his Plan. (October 5, 1864)

The first open disagreement between Cardinal Barnabo and Comboni was over the location of the Central Committee for the realization of the Plan for Africa. Barnabo was very definitely for Paris, whereas Comboni was absolutely against it, being determined "to keep his missionary activity away from any political influence (Catholic France with

England was then hunting for colonies in Africa)
and to keep absolute freedom of action!" (To Father Mazza, October 20, 1864)

What is rather amazing is that Cardinal Barnabo, with the approval of Pope Pius IX, sent Comboni
to the Propagation of the Faith in Lyons for help,
but without giving him any written recommendation; evidently he knew about the refusal Comboni
was going to get. And that is exactly what happened.
Comboni wrote immediately from Lyons to the
Cardinal: "Your Eminence was apparently aware of
the answer I was going to receive in Lyons. But I
am at peace and most pleased because everything
depends on Propaganda Fide." As we see, Comboni
was clearsighted but certainly very respectful also.
And in the same letter of December, 1864, he
begged for a written recommendation.

The answer, however, that Cardinal Barnabo
sent to Comboni at Lyons on January 17, 1865, far
from being a recommendation, sounded more like a
refusal to cooperate and a way to send Comboni's
Plan among the lost cases.

At the same time, the Cardinal wrote to Father
Mazza in Verona asking again about Comboni and
his Plan. Father Mazza replied that he knew the
Plan, liked it and that, if it were approved, he would
work for it with his Institute. As a result of this letter, Cardinal Barnabo wrote to Bishop Massaia—

then in Paris with Comboni—and spread the rumor that Comboni apparently did not belong to the Mazza Institute any more.

Because of this distrust Comboni suffered immensely to say the least. From a letter to the Cardinal (Paris, April, 1865), it is evident that his heart was bleeding, but not bitter. Africa was at stake. He could take anything and just keep going.

On June 23, 1865, he wrote again from Verona to Cardinal Barnabo making an account of all his traveling in Europe and of the good results in prospective vocations and financial help.

From now on the distrust of the Cardinal seemed to diminish as time went by. A year later, June 30, 1866, Comboni again wrote to him about his Plan for Africa, described the work accomplished so far and again asked for a letter of recommendation. It is not certain whether such a letter of recommendation ever was written. Maybe in 1868? We do know that Propaganda Fide did direct and advise Comboni on his preliminary activities in Cairo, as a first step for the realization of his Plan for the Salvation of Africa.

THE FIRST VATICAN COUNCIL

The Ecumenical Council was to be solemnly opened on December 8, 1869. Not only was the date highly significant, but for the first time in history the ill-calculated protection of "sacristan" emperors and kings was purposely refused. It was the last great gesture of the immortal Pius IX. After manifesting to his corrupt century a celestial ideal in the Immaculate Conception, after having denounced its follies in the Syllabus, the undaunted Pontiff had freed the sailing Boat of Peter once and for all from all secular interferences. And yet the general unrest in Europe seemed by all means to have created a situation which was most desperately calling for protection. But Pius IX, using this precedent, was telling the world that indeed Christ-God was powerful enough to take care of His Church.

Moreover, the fact that the beloved children gathered around him were coming from the four corners of the world proved that if anyone still entertained the obsolete idea of an infant Church, he was utterly wrong.

Only one child of the Church was missing from the Council: the African. And this was torture to Comboni. From Cairo he could not wait to tell the

Holy Father how he and his children were all and entirely with him, though unfortunately only in spirit.

On September 18, 1869, in the name of his Africans he wrote to Pope Pius IX: "Most Holy Father, on today's feast of the maternal sorrows of the Immaculate Virgin, recalling the sorrows that you yourself suffer, we come to you. . . . Although by divine will and by your own word we are so far away from you, we do not love you less for this reason nor is our devotion diminished. On the contrary, we can say in all truth that you become for us every day something more sacred, a marvel more prodigious, a love more strong. In the sad abandonment which surrounds you, your name is the sweetest of our memories, your image the most pleasant of our companions, your history the most frequent subject of our conversations. Every day we think of you, we speak of you, we pray for you. With you we suffer and never night comes without a sigh and a prayer for you by us and by our African children. Adorable Pontiff and King, may Heaven save you for many years to come for the glory of the Church, the defense of justice, the comfort of humanity . . . the prosperity of the Catholic Missions. . . . Never before has the Pontificate been so interesting to the world as in your reign, never has the Roman Pontiff ever taken God's place here on earth more universally than you. May you be blessed to live to see the ardently desired results you expect from this Ecumenical Council, inspired in you by God.

"In presenting to you, as an act of homage, the symbolic offering of 25 lires of our African children, we protest our resolution to accept with perfect obedience of will and intellect whatever decisions the Council may take, as express revelations from God, and our readiness to teach them and defend them even with our blood and our life. While we humbly beg you to present to the Council the needs of all the Catholic Missions of the world, we dare to recommend in a special manner the needs of our own unhappy Central Africa as the greatest of all and certainly the most desperate. And yet even among these Africans there are, O Holy Father, sheep that belong to Your flock; among them also there are hearts who love You. Even among the Africans—we can see it after our long experience— God is preparing for His Church and for You, His Vicar, great consolations indeed. The hour of salvation for this unfortunate people seems to have come. The cry of anguish of their centuries-old-misfortunes has already had an answer in your paternal heart. We hope that a spark of your love for Africa may be shared by all the Fathers of the Council. This is the hope of the Missionaries, the Sisters and teachers who work here in Cairo in our institutions for African boys and girls. This is the hope also of four new converts we present you today as our special gift; the hope of our First Communicants who today received Jesus for you; the hope of our catechumens who can't wait to call you 'Father.' Your blessing on our ardent desires will add to your crown the gem of a redeemed Africa."

The Ecumenical Council opened and Father Daniel followed it with prayers and crosses, "two things so dear to me!" He wrote to his Bishop Canossa in Rome urging him "to insist and raise his voice at the Council for Africa." He wrote the same to Cardinal Barnabo. But that was not enough. An occasion like this would never happen again. Somebody should go to Rome and explain in person to all the Bishops of the world the desperate problem of forgotten Africa. Comboni consulted his Missionaries. All agreed that he should go. Current events made the need for prompt action more imperative than ever.

Samuel Baker, in the name of the Kedive of Egypt, had left Cairo for Khartoum on December 5, 1869 with 2,600 men. On February 8th of the following year, Baker and his men were leaving Khartoum on thirty-three boats for the conquest of all the regions of the White Nile as far as the Equatorial Lakes.

Comboni could not wait any longer. "If there are those who can fight and die to conquer these people, what do we do to save their immortal souls?" he asked almost in tears. He wrote again to his Bishop. Canossa replied and told him to come to Rome as his personal theologian. At this news all the Missionaries were jubilant, and in March, 1870, he was in Rome. Comboni felt quite at home in the Eternal City. All the bishops and prelates he had met in his continuous traveling in Europe were at the Council; he could meet them and talk to them about Africa. He discussed matters with his very intimate friend Canon Mitterrutzner of Bressanone, who was the right hand of Monsignor Fessler, the Secretary General of the Council. It was decided that Comboni would propose to all the Fathers of the Council to sign a "Postulate" in favor of Central Africa. But to smooth the way to a favorable acceptance of the "Postulate" he first sent out a long letter in Latin overflowing with love for his Africans. Then the "Postulate" followed.

Very briefly he explained that, although a few missions had been established along part of the coasts of Africa, all the interior, in spite of heroic efforts, was still with no apostles, no churches, no faith. Through their bishops the faithful of the world were going to be made acquainted with its dire needs. All the undersigned fathers at the Council were desperately pleading with all the Ordinaries of the world to give a chance to these some hundred millions of Africans who were knocking insistently at the door of the Church. And he concluded: "On the refulgent crown decked with celestial diamonds which adorns the august head of the triumphant and Immaculate Mother of God, may Africa, conquered for Christ, shine as the dark gem."

The "Postulate" was signed by 70 Patriarchs, Archbishops and Bishops; among them the four Bishops of the United States: M. J. Spalding of Baltimore, J. B. Purcell of Cincinnati, W. H. Elder of Natches and J. Bayley Roosevelt of Newark. Pius IX signed it July 18, 1870, the same day of the definition of the Papal Infallibility, and he gave orders to put it among the subjects to be discussed by the Council in the sections regarding the Missions.

When the good news reached Cairo all rejoiced exceedingly. Three little girls newly baptized called on Father Carcereri and giving him each a silver franc said: "Father, this is for Our Lord, the Pope in Rome."

"Why?" Father asked.

"Because he helps us so much!"

ON THE GO

All seemed to be progressing very satisfactorily at the Ecumenical Council when on September 20, 1870, the troops of the anticlerical Italian government rather ingloriously occupied the Eternal City. The status of free sovereigns enjoyed by the Popes over a thousand years had temporarily come to an end. [1]

With the occupation of Rome the first Vatican Council was suspended indefinitely. Africa had to wait again.

Poor Comboni! Were some "inspired" friends then right who kept repeating that it was all useless, that Africa was a lost cause?

No, that could not be. He had too many proofs to the contrary. Mysteriously but truly all God's enterprises must look as "lost" at one time or another. The most striking example of all is Calvary. But Calvary was not a failure as none of God's work can ever be.

To all this Comboni had only one answer: "Africa or Death!"

---

[1] This condition was to last until Feb. 11, 1929, when Cardinal Gasparri, Secretary of State for Pius XI, and Mussolini, Prime Minister for King Victor Emmanuel III, signed the Lateran Treaty. With the creation of Vatican City the Popes regained their independence.

Indeed his physical endurance and will-power seem to have something of the super-human. Above all, his trust in God, he reminds himself, must be absolutely boundless. Africa or death! Africa has not come yet, but neither death, so . . . he has to go, to try again and keep trying. Another strategic retreat, the study of new plans and, by January, 1871, he is on the move again.

He has to provide for his institutions in Cairo, which financially count exclusively on him, and above all he must have all the moral and material support he can get to reopen his seminary in Verona, dead with dear Dal Bosco's death. Now is the time. From January to August he visits one by one all the main cities of north Europe: Bolzano, Merano, Innsbruck, Munich, Altotting, Salisburg, Passau, Linz, Paderborn, Dresden, Bamberg, Fulden, Cologne, and above all Vienna. At times he feels tired, exhausted, but he has to go and he keeps going.

He is careful to keep his bishop always informed of the results of his begging, and his letters show all his love for God, Africa and crosses. Particularly in the beginning of this trip he receives few promises, some good words and many refusals and humiliations. How many times when opening his mail he reads the words of Judas: "Why all this waste?"

To Canossa once he writes: "No danger for me of being proud. God makes me bow under so many humiliations, mortifications, and denials that I cannot even have a temptation of pride. But God is right in doing so; otherwise this donkey would raise his head."

In his trials, however, he is not downcast or discouraged. In May, 1871, he writes again to his Bishop: "I adore the loving bounty of God Who gives me the blessing of so many crosses and leads me through the rugged path of Calvary.... Knowing a little, by now, the ways of Divine Providence and how God builds His works at the foot of the cross, I see as clear as the light of the sun, the dawn of great consolations to prepare our weakness for bigger crosses and more furious storms for the salvation of Africa."

For the money he needs so badly he is again calling on St. Joseph, the official Bursar of all his institutions.

"Yesterday, March 19th," he writes, "has been a happy day because I could talk very plainly to St. Joseph. At times I have to be a little bold with the Blessed Bursar of mine."

And the dear Saint never failed him.

Little by little through letters, conferences, and personal contacts things started rolling again. From January to May of this year alone (1871) he wrote 1,347 letters! Among his new friends are the Apostolic Nuncio and the Archbishop of Vienna; the Duke of Modena and also Count Chambord of France. One day he received in the mail one hundred silver talers from an anonymous donor in north Germany. The King of Hanover, a Protestant, sent him a nice donation with a letter of praise for his good work for Africa.

But what filled the heart of this tireless beggar for Africa with gratitude was the promise of the Society of Mary of Vienna to pass to him all its receipts as soon as he could get the mission of Central Africa.

"There is still hope for Africa, through your wise Plan," the Cardinal of Vienna told him. The Society of Cologne, an old friend of Comboni, gave him 20,000 francs and promised all its income for six consecutive years.

Father Daniel also cherished the thought of a trip to the United States of America. At the Vatican Council he had made friends among the American Bishops, and he was sure of getting help from their generosity. "With the help of God," he wrote to his Bishop, "I am sure I will bring you back 500,000 francs. And with that money we will work miracles for Africa." Canossa advised him, however, against such a long trip. Comboni promptly obeyed as always and turned to east Europe instead. He visited Hungary, Poland, and Russia, reaching Moscow and Petrograd.

In November, 1871, after almost a year he was back in Verona happy to "put on his Bishop's desk 80,000 lires." In those times that was no small amount of money!

"The requirements for making a good beggar," he wrote jokingly to Father Bricolo, "are three: prudence, patience, and boldness. I don't have the first one, but I have enough of the second and plenty of the third."

The humble beggar for Christ was alway so clever at covering up his virtue with jokes and hearty laughs.

A SEMINARY FOR CENTRAL AFRICA

Cardinal Barnabo used to tell Comboni: "Either you bring me here a testimonial which assures me that you will live for thirty-five years or more, or you have to establish your seminary in Verona. In either case I will give you a mission in Central Africa. Otherwise I am afraid that all your work is going to die with you." The Cardinal was speaking in a facetious tone, but he certainly meant every word of it and Father Daniel knew it.

"Now, since I have not found any Saint yet," he used to comment, "who can assure me of how long I will live, I have to get busy with the seminary. Though I am deeply convinced that I am good for nothing and that whatever I do ends in a mess, still I see how his Eminence is right."

Before leaving for his last long trip through north-east Europe, he had charged the Rector of the diocesan seminary of Verona to buy a piece of property that he himself had looked over and liked because it was very close to the diocesan seminary. Notified of the conclusion of the deal, he was happy to send 20,000 lires from Prague to pay for it. The money was a donation of the ex-emperor Ferdinand and his wife. In sending it, Daniel wrote to the Bishop: "We have to thank God and our good Bur-

121

sar St. Joseph who really wants to save the Africans
. . . I did not expect the full amount, but the Infant
of Prague was really good . . . your Excellency can
see how God wants our work for Africa . . ."

But naturally the most important problem of
all was to find men capable and willing to conduct
the seminary itself. He knew very well three young
priests of the diocesan seminary of Verona: Fathers
Fiorentini, Bacilieri and Casella. They were profes-
sors respectively of moral theology, dogmatic theology and philosophy. When the young men were
studying in Rome at the Capranica College, Comboni used to visit with them. Father Bacilieri, later
Bishop of Verona and Cardinal, always remembered
how Father Daniel invariably ended his visit with:
". . . at any rate, dear Barth, Africa or death!"

The three young men were delighted at Comboni's proposal and Father Bacilieri most willingly
agreed to be Rector, Father Fiorentini, Spiritual
Director, and Father Casella, Bursar.

When Father Daniel bravely called on Bishop
Canossa to acquaint him with the agreement, the
good Bishop was rather surprised and exclaimed:
"Good Father Daniel, do you want to rob me of the
three best men I have?"

The Bishop, nevertheless, was careful about
finding the man he was sure was going to answer
all the requirements for such a difficult task. He
was a very pious and learned young priest living
unnoticed as assistant of St. Paul Church in town:

Father Anthony Squaranti. The humble and prudent priest was disturbed and afraid of such an assignment, but finally he gave in to his Bishop's will recognizing in it the will of God.

Bishop Canossa proceeded to the canonical erection of the seminary for the Missions of Central Africa with a decree dated December 8, 1871. In the same decree he also approved the rules on a trial basis, as is the custom of the Church in such cases. The rules were the result of Father Daniel's many years of study and prayer together with his missionary experience and many personal contacts with other institutions in his continual travelling.

"The seminary," he wrote, "is first of all subject to the Vicar of Christ and to the Sacred Congregation of Propaganda Fide always and in everything. . . .

"The greatest care must be used in accepting aspirants. . . . Their vocation must be carefully studied and they have to be told in no uncertain terms how sublime their vocation is and how extremely difficult is going to be their apostolate for which the most proved virtue is required. A mediocre one is only bound to fail. . . . No vain or selfish motives should prompt anyone to join this Institute. . . . The pure glory of God and the salvation of souls must be their only recompense. . . .

"The aspirants will begin their period of formation with a ten-day retreat during which a general confession is advisable. Soon after, the two-year

novitiate begins. The novitiate period is to be entirely dedicated to acquiring a genuine spirit of
prayer, self-denial and love for sacrifice. As for the
method to be used in the novitiate, the rules of the
Society of Jesus should be followed as much as
possible. . . .

"The daily spiritual exercises will consist in a
one-hour meditation in the morning, Holy Mass, a
fifteen-minute examination of conscience before
lunch and before rest in the evening; holy Rosary,
visit to the Blessed Sacrament and spiritual reading.
There will also be a weekly confession, a monthly
day of recollection, and ten days of retreat every
year. . . ."

Many other practical counsels were given, but
the main idea was always on sacrifice as the Number
One requirement for a missionary vocation. On occasion he did not hesitate to dramatize the fact.
For example, the Rev. Father Moreno, Pastor of
Gaino on the Lake Garda, had expressed the ardent
desire to go to Africa with Comboni. The latter arranged for an appointment in Limone, at the house
of his own father. To the surprise of the good priest,
whom apparently Comboni knew very well, he had
a dinner ready for him consisting only of corn meal
and dry figs.

"You see," he commented to his wide-eyed
guest, "I eat a little worse than this in Africa, just
plain grains of durra or something of the like. Of

course here," he concluded with a fine smile, "Divine Providence lets us eat a little better!" Other things were discussed and the result of the interview was, "Sorry, Father, you are not cut out for Africa!"

Father Daniel in spite of his terrific activity kept himself always very close to his co-workers in the seminary. He was always so understanding and so encouraging. "Do not let yourself be overcome with tediousness," he wrote to one. "Keep in mind that you are forming apostles and perhaps martyrs. . . ."

But above all he himself was a living example of prayer and sacrifice. When he was at home, his punctuality at the community exercises was exemplary. During his long traveling he was always in prayer. And apparently that was not enough, because he also used to pray long hours at night. How many times he was caught in prayer in his room till very late hours, or seen down in the garden walking under the stars with the Rosary in his hand. Prayer was the breath of his life.

He also encouraged the reception of Holy Communion as often as possible and used to suggest a very short formula for spiritual communions during the day: "My God, I love You; in my heart I want You!"

Knowing human nature so well, he did his best to keep his young men from getting discouraged.

"Don't be surprised at ingratitude or lack of success!
The less men pay, the more God pays. . . . All missionaries must go to heaven because they sacrifice
everything for the salvation of souls. . . . Even only
one soul saved is the greatest recompense to all
sacrifices, no matter how big! . . ."

He ardently desired to have a Jesuit Father as
Master of his Novices, but all he could get from the
General of that venerable Order was a promise.
Four years after his death he would see from heaven
his dream come true.

A Shilluk warrior, Sudan

A Shilluk canoe

Jur warriors, "first cousins" of the Shilluks

The tombs of the Missionaries of Gondokoro

Bishop Massaia and Young Father Comboni—Paris, France

The beginning of Comboni's buildings in Cairo, Egypt

3

SCARLET SUNSET

1872-1881

ROME HAS SPOKEN

When in November 1871, the Council of the Association of the Good Shepherd presided over by Canossa agreed that the time for a mission had come, Comboni moved to Rome where he remained working tirelessly until the historic May, 1872. The proverbial "Eternal" Rome was naturally too slow for Comboni. One day he said to Cardinal Barnabo: "For God's sake, your Eminence, let us hurry because my poor Africans are going to hell...." To whom the Cardinal answered with a smile: "My dear Comboni, your Africans have waited for 4,000 years, they can wait for a few more months."

At last in May, 1872, the Sacred Congregation of the Cardinals of Propaganda Fide in a Plenary Session deliberated to entrust the Vicariate Apostolic of Central Africa to Comboni and his new Institute. Comboni was to be in charge as Pro-Vicar Apostolic.

Five days later, Pope Pius IX confirmed the decision. Father Daniel jubilantly wrote to Bishop Canossa: "We asked for a mission in Central Africa and the Holy See gave us all Central Africa erected in an independent vicariate!"

The news spread rapidly all over Europe bringing immense joy to all Comboni's friends. After so

many years of work and suffering, God was rewarding His faithful servant. But if Comboni is overflowing with joy, there is no room for complacency
in his great heart. He repeats again and again that
the salvation of Africa can be accomplished only by
the Cross, and he prays to Jesus for some big one.
"The hundred millions of Africans will be conquered
not by the brutal force of armies, but by that sweet
power which emanated from the Crucified God,
Who embraced with His open arms all the world."

After taking care of some business in Southern
Italy, he was in Vienna on September 5. The Emper-
or Francis Joseph received him with great honor,
and since Egypt was still under Turkish dominion, he
obtained for him letters from the Sultan of Con-
stantinople for the Kedive of Egypt and all the
Pashas of the Sudan. From Vienna, the Pro-Vicar
was back in Verona. On September 17, the ceremony
of the departure was held in Bishop Canossa's private chapel. The following day, Comboni left for
Trieste with four priests, three brothers, and three
African teachers. On September 26, they arrived in
Cairo where everybody was anxiously waiting for the
new Pro-Vicar Apostolic of Central Africa. Four
months were spent in diligent preparations. At last
the long-awaited day arrived. It was January 26,
1873. After having imparted benediction with the
Most Blessed Sacrament, Comboni delivered the

farewell sermon to all present. All were in tears, but those who wept most were the missionaries and African teachers who could not leave with him now.

More than a sermon, Comboni's was the "Pep-talk" of a general just before a decisive battle. Fifteen years had passed since he has left Cairo for Khartoum the first time. How much brighter things looked now; his genial plan was already bearing fruit both in Verona and Cairo. Many friends were financially behind him in Europe and above all Comboni himself had matured, with an unmatched experience, under the ever-present blessing of his ardently-desired, everyday cross. After the Papal blessing the Pro-Vicar lead a huge crowd to the Nile. Among thunderous shouts of "Long live Pius IX, Long live Comboni," the two big boats started moving slowly up the calm Nile. Comboni and his twenty co-workers, priests, sisters and African teachers, looked like a party leaving for a pleasure trip, whereas they very well knew that the Sudan was still the "inferno" De Jacobis spoke of some twenty years before.

The longest non-stop stretch from Cairo to Shellal was made in thirty-seven days. One sister who had become very ill was cured by Comboni's fervent prayer.

The second stop, Korosco, was much closer, but at Shellal the Nile enters into the desert and the traveling becomes monotonous and at times melancholic. It took only eight days from Shellal to Koros-co. In this big village, our missionaries disembarked from the boats of the Nile to mount the "Ships of the Desert" the patient, marvelous camels. The Pro-Vicar got some fifty of them for the crossing of the Korosco desert, which by forced marches was done in only six days. At times, they traveled even seventeen hours a day. At Abu-Hamed the Nile appeared again and they coasted to Berber. From this small town they set out by boat again, and arrived in Khartoum on May 4, 1873, exactly ninety-nine days after leaving Cairo.

The arrival of the Pro-Vicar in the Capitol of the Sudan was a real triumph. Father Carereri had carefully prepared every detail for the warmest welcome. The civil authorities were present also. The church celebrations were kept for the following Sunday. Comboni offered the Divine Sacrifice and delivered the sermon:

"I cannot express in words how happy I am to be back with you after long, trying years. The first love of my youth has been for Central Africa. Sixteen years ago I left father and mother and everything to come here to spend my life for you; but the difficult climate of the White Nile at Holy Cross got the best of me. Obedience sent me home but my heart remained here. As soon as I recovered, all my thoughts, plans, and continuous traveling were for you. And now at last I return to you to take back my heart only to open it wider, if possible, to love you as your spiritual father. . . . I come back to you to be always yours, vowed to your good forever. Day and night, sun and rain will find me equally ready to minister to your needs. . . . Your good will be my good, your sorrows, my sorrows. Your cause from now on will be my cause and the happiest day will be the one on which I am allowed to give my life for you. I am well aware of the fact that my task will be a hard one. Sent by the Holy See to be your shepherd and teacher, I have to protect you, to teach you, to correct you. It is my ardent prayer that no one will ever take offense, but on the contrary, will understand my fatherly heart and help me to love you. . . . My greeting and my thanks to all my valiant co-operators; the Rev. Father Carcereri, my able Vicar General, the missionaries, sisters and African teachers. We are all united to work and die for your salvation. And now my thought goes to you, O most merciful Queen of Africa. You are the loving Mother of all this Vicariate and we are all your children. . . . O Mary, Mother of God, the greatest part of your African children live still in the 'darkness and in the shadow of death.' Hasten the hour of salvation. . . . Keep sending new apostles to this country, so much in need and in sorrow. . . ."

SLAVERY

Comboni cut short the celebrations and proceeded to reorganize the Catholic Mission in Khartoum. He contacted the few Catholics, about one hundred out of 50,000 inhabitants, most of them "living like Turks," and immediately took care to have two schools started, one for boys and one for girls. Pro-Vicar Knoblecher in 1854-56 had erected a big building all in stone, which was still in a very good condition.

After a month Comboni was ready to leave for El-Obeid, the capital of the Kordofan province. This was a large city of about 100,000 people. Three quarters were Africans, most of them slaves.

Two years before when Comboni ordered Carcereri to move from Cairo into the interior to Kordofan and look for a suitable place for a mission, Father Carcereri had chosen El-Obeid. Situated in the midst of a large forest and with plenty of good water it was an ideal spot from the health standpoint, but the real fame of this "great metropolis" was due to the fact that it was the very heart of the slave market of all the Sudan.

As in Khartoum, the new Pro-Vicar had a tremendous reception in El-Obeid also. The governor of Kordofan thought it was politically wise not to be second to his superior of Khartoum, so he was very careful to be there in person with two generals, all the civil authorities, and even the garrison's band. But there was more than that. The very day Comboni was entering El-Obeid, the great Pasha solemnly proclaimed the abolition of slavery. He himself let over two hundred of his slaves go free and closed the city's slave market, always well filled with "thousands" of Africans waiting to be sold.

As in Khartoum, Comboni showed the greatest appreciation for all that was done in his honor by the authorities, but, by no means was he being fooled by them. He knew very well that the Pashas and all their subordinates, from the first to the last, were cordially united against him and would have done anything to destroy him and the Catholic Mission. But they were afraid of "this terrific man" who had behind him not only Europe but apparently even the Kedive of Cairo. The Pro-Vicar realized that he had the initiative, and cautiously, with supreme tact, he proceeded to exploit the situation in favor of the most unhappy of all mankind, the slaves.

He thought that by avoiding the White Nile he had steered clear of hideous "merchants of human beings" who were the main obstacle to Faith and civilization, but he realized that it was not so. Indeed such a place did not exist in Central Africa. At least 5,000 slave traders were operating there. Romolo Gessi, the implacable fighter of these execrable monsters, estimated that some 100,000 Africans had been taken from his area every year and sold like cattle in Egypt and elsewhere. and of course, many thousands more had died. The man-hunt was in full swing, contrary to the ultra-simple and altogether misleading statement of Baker.

Comboni himself, coming from Cairo to Khar-toum in April, 1873, saw over forty boats filled to capacity with slaves, and about twenty long cara-vans going to Egypt. In June of the same year, be-tween the White Nile and El-Obeid only, he met thousands of slaves, mostly boys and girls, bound with chains and ropes and pushed forward like cattle. This is what he and his missionaries would see every day from now on. Ironically, at the same time newspapers all over the world were writing big articles about slavery being completely sup-pressed. The tragic truth was that Africa was "bleeding from all its pores."

As an apostle of Christ and representative of the angelical Pius IX, Comboni was determined to supplant the secular kingdom of Satan, whose su-preme law is hatred without limit, with the super-natural kingdom of Christ whose supreme law is love.

His first official act as the head of the Vicariate of Central Africa was the consecration of the entire mission to the Sacred Heart of Jesus held on the feast of the Exaltation of the Holy Cross. The infinite love of the Savior of all men was going to lead him and his missionaries successfully toward the destruction of the abominable cancer of Central Africa: slavery.

"I am trying to find out," wrote Comboni to a friend in Austria, "the way to put our mission in a position to force the government and the Pashas to do something real and practical to diminish the torture of these most unhappy ones (the slaves). And I see that the authorities are afraid of the Catholic Mission. Whatever slaves I find, I take to the officials and I have them freed. . . ."

Unfortunately, many supposed Catholics were involved in the infamous trade. As head of the Church in the Sudan, Comboni, therefore, wrote a pastoral letter in which, after having called the attention of the Catholics on certain serious abuses, he stigmatized with the most scorching words, any direct or indirect co-operation with the abominable and inhuman slave trade. He defended the human dignity of all Africans and their right to the Christian family. After having recalled the various condemnations of slavery by the Popes, he forbade any co-operation whatsoever in the trading of slaves, and reminded those who already had them of their strict obligation to treat them as human beings and to give them the chance to study the true religion. For backsliders, he threatened recourse to the literal application of the Egyptian laws on the matter, which of course, had only been on the paper till then.

His pastoral letter was read in all the churches with very good results. "It scared not only Catholics, but Protestants and Turks as well."

Comboni knew, of course, that to free as many slaves as possible was not enough. It was also necessary to provide them with a place where they could be vocationally trained to earn a decent living. For this purpose, he bought a large piece of fertile land with water at Malbes, a few miles from El-Obeid. In a very short time, a model village was born there made up of all Catholic families. There was Mass in the morning and all gathered together for the Rosary in the evening. Incidentally, this was part of his famous "plan."

All this was something, but it was far from being enough. Writing at this time to Cardinal Barnabo, Comboni expressed his larger hopes: "With the help of God, the Church, little by little, perhaps will succeed in what the 'great powers' of Europe most certainly have not done yet, namely, in completely abolishing this infamous slavery among these Africans."

As positive a man as he was, Comboni, however, far from flattering himself, was expecting in the near future a strong reaction against the Church, the number one enemy of slavery. Therefore, if he imposed on himself the strict rule of always proceeding with the greatest "prudence" and "cautiousness," he did not, on the other hand, want to be alone in such a terrific endeavor. Very frequently he called on the Holy See for advice and submitted everything to the "wisdom of the Sacred Congregation of Propaganda Fide before taking any important step."

Besides this personal contact with Rome, he instructed Father Carcereri to put in writing a complete report on slavery in the Sudan. The report was checked point by point by Comboni and all the missionaries, "to be sure that everything was according to the exact truth." Then he sent Carcereri himself to Rome and Vienna to speak the whole truth about slavery and to solicit all the support he could get in fighting it to the end.

This was a very intelligent move on the part of Comboni, because after the first years of co-operation, the Egyptian government and even the Austrian consul (to whom the Holy See had directed to appeal) were more or less openly siding with the masters of the slaves against the slaves and, of course, against justice. The law was that the slaves should be returned if the master requested them.

The missionaries could not always keep silent before these facts and, unfortunately, now and then someone went too far, committing real imprudences in the matter.

The poor Pro-Vicar would then, as usual, have the unpleasant task of answering for it. That meant that he had to do rather difficult and different things at one and the same time, such as saving the Catholic

Mission, keeping his task as patron of the slaves and somehow trying to defend, or at least excuse his missionaries. And with God's help he always succeeded.

One time, during the absence of Comboni, things went so badly that even General Gordon, then governor of the Sudan and an intimate friend of Comboni, had recourse to the Holy See against the missionaries. Comboni was then in Rome and was immediately called by the Cardinal Prefect of Propaganda Fide. He plainly stated to the Cardinal that General Gordon was really a good man who was trying sincerely to fight slavery; in fact, he had forbidden the Mohammedan Baggaras, under the most severe punishments, to raid the pagan tribes and he had ordered the latter in turn to pay their tribute not in slaves but in money or cattle. On the other hand, Comboni also reminded Rome not to forget in what kind of extremely trying predicament his missionaries were living every single day, for long, long years. At any rate, he submitted once more the directives given by him to his missionaries, and once more he asked Propaganda Fide for some concrete rules and suggestions on the matter. He also could not hide the fact that about four-fifths of the slaves the Mission was protecting kept living an immoral life, and, on the other hand, the hatred of the Mohammedans against the Christians was mounting frightfully. "In my judgment, since the unjust laws concerning the return of slaves to their masters are going to last only twelve more years, it might be wiser not to irritate the Mohammedan masters excessively and follow the reasonable suggestions of General Gordon. What counts above all is that the Holy See may be able to keep the Catholic Mission in the Sudan, which at the present, is more important than a few conversions."

The proverbial zeal of Comboni was indeed mingled with wisdom and prudence. What if the missionaries had to be expelled from the Sudan? Who could ever defend in the least the poor slaves? It was better to be satisfied with just a little for the present, praying and working hard to have more and perhaps everything in the future.

And so he continued to help in every possible way the oppressed and the poor. Thus he could write: "At the sight of so many horrors and miseries my missionaries are determined to sacrifice their very lives for the salvation of these most unfortunate people. We don't feel the equatorial heat nor the privations of this most difficult mission; neither the fatigue of journeys, nor the uncomfortable huts or the lack of everything. We have disposed of our underwear and sheets and necessaries in order to give a piece of something to the women we freed from slavery. We all are determined to suffer anything to better the condition of these Africans and to call them to our Faith. Our war cry to the very last breath will be 'Africa or Death!' The Sacred Heart will triumph."

FREEDOM ON THE MOUNTAINS

Comboni had heard so much of the Nubans who because of their persistent rejection of Islamism were often massacred by the ferocious Giallabas and other slave traders. Now in El-Obeid he could personally meet many of them. All in town were speaking so highly of these mountaineers as the best servants, so faithful and industrious. From among the Nuban slaves so often brought to El-Obeid the government was also recruiting the best soldiers.

Through a government official, Comboni succeeded in having a visit with the Nuban chief, Said Aga. It was the feast of Our Lady of Mount Carmel. The man was spellbound on seeing the chapel, the school, the trade school, and he was particularly moved by the warm, paternal welcome of Comboni who went so far as to expressing his desire to found a mission among the Nuban tribe.

Back home, Said's people could not believe all those wonderful things, but Said at least succeeded in convincing the great chief Cakum to come to El-Obeid to see for himself. On the feast of Our Lady of Ransom, the great Cakum with twenty men arrived at Comboni's residence. That was the most memorable day of the chief's whole life. The trade school attracted him most. To see African children do all those wonderful things was just unbelievable. He wanted to touch everything: hoses, spades, hammers, nails, saws, axes, planes. But what really fascinated him was the harmonium. When Comboni played a piece for him, Cakum and his men exclaimed: "Marvelous! You know everything, you work miracles!" Of course, he wanted to try too, but naturally nothing came out. "You are the son of God," he cried out. "From a piece of wood you can get voices which are more harmonious than those of the birds of the forest."

Comboni took him to the Sisters' house and showed him Sister Faustina, an ex-Nuban girl, trained in Italy, who knew how to sew and knit and could recite wonderful prayers.

"No mortal is greater and more able than you!" observed the great chief.

"Oh yes," replied Comboni promptly. "There are many Christians in Europe who know more than I do. They even gave me money to help the Africans. First of all, and above all there is the great wise Priest, the good and glorious Chief of all Christians, the Vicar of God on earth. This great Chief and Priest is the one who loves you most. He sent me and my companions here to help you spiritually and materially so you may know the truth and be happy."

The Nubans exclaimed: "A marvelous thing! The great Priest thinks of us from far away!"

Then Comboni showed them the little library and finally he asked Cakum to say something which Comboni wrote on a piece of paper and read back to him. The good man remained speechless, but after a while he dared to ask: "Does the great Priest from far away know how to write too?" Comboni showed his Moroni's Ecclesiastical Encyclopedia and said emphatically: "Look here, great chief, do you see all these books? Well, the son of the barber of the great Priest (for such was Moroni) wrote all these! Now think if the great priest himself does not know how to write!"

"We are all ignorant," said Cakum striking his forehead with his hand. "We don't know a thing, we are like animals. Come to our villages and teach us all this. I string my cow or camel to the right and they go right. I tell my servant to lead the oxen and my slaves to fetch the water and they do it. Tell us what path to follow and we will obey you like servants and slaves. We, our wives, our children, our servants, our slaves, our oxen, our cows, our goats, our sheep, our land, our cabins, our crops and even the leaves of our trees will all be yours We will be your children and slaves, you will be our father and master of all."

Comboni entertained Chief Cakum and his men for four days.

On leaving, the great Nuban said: "The Mohammedans tried to tell us that Christians are bad, that they eat the heart, the liver and the brains of

men, but I always knew that they were wrong. . . .
There are not in the whole world people more sacred
than you and your companions. We will obey you;
you are children of heaven and of God."

Comboni wanted to go in person to visit the
Nubans, but being too busy in El-Obeid he sent
three of the missionaries to explore the Nuban region. They came back all enthusiastic after fifteen
days, suggesting Delen as a suitable place for a
mission.

Comboni, however, did not have a single man
at his disposal for the moment, so painfully he waited
for the first occasion.

A short time later, while going back to Khartoum on camel-back, his animal, frightened by a hy-
ena that unexpectedly came out from behind a bush,
went wild and threw him to the ground. When
Comboni, after thirty hours, came to his senses, he
found himself under a tent that his missionaries had
pitched for him. Blood was coming out of his mouth
and his left arm was broken. After a few days, although still in terrible pain, he could mount the
camel again. After four interminable days, he
arrived in Khartoum. Only after three months could
he use his left arm again.

In Khartoum, he provided a much-needed new
house for the sisters. Notifying Propaganda Fide, he
wrote: "Before leaving El-Obeid, I charged my
bursar, St. Joseph, for this business and he certainly
is doing fine! In only fifteen days, he brought me

almost 35,000 francs in gold, not bad at all. . . .
Central Africa needs a fantastic amount of money,
but in St. Joseph, we have a top administrator and
the Sacred Heart of Jesus is rich in both mercy and
money. . . ."

In a few months the sisters were living in the
new house. At this time he also gave orders to set
up new buildings in better positions, for his institutions in Cairo. In this work, Comboni was evidently heaven-inspired, for without these firm bases in
Egypt the African Missions would have certainly
been destroyed after Comboni's death.

Good news also came from the new governor
general of the Sudan, Colonel Gordon, who assured
Comboni of an expedition to the Equatorial Lakes.

"After Gebel-Nuba, the great lakes at the
equator. . . ." wrote Comboni, December 19, 1874, to
Propaganda. But the best news of all was of Father
Carcereri's arrival from Europe with new missionaries.

The Pro-Vicar's first thought was for the dear
Nubans. He at once sent two priests, two brothers,
and a well-trained Nuban there. Later in June, he
left Khartoum for El-Obeid and Gebel-Nuba. The
governor's steamer took him and his companions to
Tura and from there they took twenty-six camels
to El-Obeid, where he entered, at the ringing of the
bells, amid the joy of the Catholics and particularly of his African children. The governor sent a

white horse for Monsignor Pro-Vicar so he could enter the town like a great man, under arches of green, and of "as much red as they could find."

On September 15, twelve camels were readied and he left for Gebel-Nuba with a small group of missionaries, among them two sisters. After five days he met a ferocious Baggara in the forest, to whom he presented a nice piece of silk and sent him to tell the chief Cakum of his arrival. The meeting that followed in the forest was most fascinating. They both exchanged gifts, had a nice supper, and all slept under the stars. Around noon of the following day Comboni entered Delen on the horse of the great chief among shouts of joy from the whole population.

Comboni was happy. At last his dream of a real mission in the interior had come true. But strange enough, on this very occasion, he was writing to Propaganda: "God wants to save this unhappy Africa. Now we wait for more crosses. . . . May God help us to die for His love and the salvation of these people. He died for them, too."

And the crosses came soon. Thirteen of the fifteen missionaries took sick, and he was among the first. Worst of all, a note came from the governor of El-Obeid to move out of Delen because he knew of an attack planned by Mohammedan Baggaras against the Nubans. Comboni tipped the messenger nicely and he got quite another story out of him. The governor himself was in the forest with a thousand soldiers and four canons ready to raid the Nubans and get all the slaves he wanted. Comboni was desperate, but he could neither call Khartoum in such a short time, nor could he persuade the governor to desist. After a quick meeting with his missionaries, they concluded that there was only one thing to do, to move out. The governor was diabolically kind enough to send some twenty camels to hasten their departure. Comboni did not say "Good-bye," but "We'll be seeing you soon."

It was a battle lost at an awful price, but the war was not over. He was determined to carry it on till the end and destroy, at least among the Nubans, at any price that shame of mankind, slavery. Comboni left orders for his missionaries to go back to Delen as soon as possible. Nearly two long years passed, but finally they did return and this time to stay. The Nubans themselves came to El-Obeid to take them back in triumph. The Baggaras regarded the Catholic Mission as a "stone on their heart."

One day a big chief of this ferocious Mohammedan tribe thus addressed the local governor of El-Obeid: "If you leave these dogs of Christians at Gebel-Nuba, we cannot pay our taxes anymore because we will not be able to go up there to take our 'chickens' (slave children), our 'goats' (young slaves), and our 'camels' (adult slaves). Chickens, goats and camels were the usual terms used even in the official books of the governor of El-Obeid to cover up the infamous truth.

The Mohammedan slave merchants had now grounds for complaint. Since the Catholic Mission was in Delen not a single slave had been captured from the mountains. The rules given here by the Pro-Vicar were quite different than those for the Mohammedan regions. "In Gebel-Nuba and in all places not directly under the Egyptian government, we must make every possible effort to create the 'right of asylum' for the fugitive slaves, knowing that in those primitive tribes the Church is 'law maker.' In practice we have to apply the laws and the spirit of the Gospel and of the Church and therefore protect the interests of the slave, at any cost before any chief and governor."

After awhile, however, the Baggara slave hunters started all over again. The missionaries told Comboni about it and he lost no time. His ascendancy iver the Kedive in Cairo and over the governor general in Khartoum, Rauf Pasha, was at an all-time high. He immediately contacted Rauf who gave him a very peppery letter for the governor of El-Obeid. Then Comboni left for Delen determined to end the story once and forever and to give those "robbers and assassins" to the authorities to be judged.

Somehow, the news that he was coming to Kordofan with full powers from Cairo and Khartoum leaked out and spread terror among the slave traders, from the local governor down.

As soon as he arrived in El-Obeid, all of them competed with one another in inviting him to big dinners. Comboni never refused and thus succeeded in fooling them beautifully.

"Among these hideous merchants of human beings there are millionaires," wrote Comboni to Propaganda, 1881. "One is Tefaala, who stole Daniel Sorur, now studying for the priesthood in Rome. There is another one whom the governor made 'pasha' for his merits as a slave trader. He has some thousand slaves at his orders and forty-two children; he can give each one of the latter about about 260,000 golden francs, that is about eleven million in all."

The great chief of the Nubans and the missionaries met the Pro-Vicar immediately after his arrival in El-Obeid and reconfirmed the charge that the Baggaras were still stealing children and crops. Comboni asked governor general Rauf Pasha for soldiers. The good Pasha immediately sent one hundred men assuring him that he was willing to give him a thousand, if he wished it. Above all he sent a letter charging Comboni to examine the whole situation and to suggest appropriate remedies.

This letter can be called the glorious victory of Comboni in his tireless war against slavery.

On May 24, Comboni initiated his exploration among the Nubans. The poor governor of El-Obeid gave him his own horse and six cavalrymen as escort. The indefatigable Pro-Vicar passed from mountain to mountain, from village to village and all his notes are but a long litany of "killing . . . massacring . . . robbing . . . destroying. . . ." and the like.

Every place he stopped, chiefs and people fell at Comboni's feet imploring to be freed from the slave traders, by whom they were on the verge of being almost completely destroyed. With all his big heart he consoled them, weeping with them, promising speedy and concrete help. And the poor, good, unfortunate people showed him their children, their huts and fields, crying with joy and proclaiming him their savior.

Comboni hurried his report to the governor general who sent a French inspector and fresh troops right away. A Baggara chief was killed and another put in jail. This was just the beginning. Giegler Pasha was subsequently sent from Khartoum to arrest all the chief slave traders, hang some, seize all the horses of the Baggaras and take any necessary measure. Thus the Pro-Vicar in a letter to his father: "I just related the pure truth about hundreds of criminals who became rich with the blood of these dear Nubans, selling and ruining their young people by the thousands. . . . The governor is of the opinion that only force can stop that. Well, that is his business. As for myself I think he is right. Let the assassins be hanged and the innocent live. . . ."

Following Comboni's suggestion, governor general Rauf was planning to create a separate province for the Nubans under an "honest" governor from Europe.

Six years later, in 1881, as the last step to eradicate slavery, Comboni suggested a railroad from the Red Sea to Khartoum. He kept repeating insistently: "A railroad in the Sudan means the end of slavery." In order to succeed in his intent and to put more pressure on Cairo's and Khartoum's officials, he reminded them also of the immense material advantages which such a railroad would bring to Egypt and to the Sudan. The Kedive was in favor of it and Rauf Pasha was enthusiastic.

Moreover, Comboni had succeeded in convincing the French consul and Paris to add their good services in pushing towards the realization of the great project.

All seemed to indicate that Comboni was going to be successful also in this last of his dreams against the abominable slavery. But for God, the indefatigable servant had worked enough and He called Comboni to his reward.

"MOTHERS OF THE AFRICANS"

Khartoum, December 8, 1875: Pro-Vicar Comboni solemnly consecrated the vicariate of Central Africa to Our Lady of the Sacred Heart. At the end of his first visit to Gebel-Nuba he had written to all the churches of the mission to make the ceremony as solemn as possible, enclosing the prayer that he himself had composed for the occasion. In it he desperately calls on the Immaculate Virgin Mother of God "To come and reign in these desolate lands. . . . You only can give to so many millions, in suffering and sorrow, their Lord and their God. . . . After Jesus, you are all our hope . . . after Jesus, you are everything for us . . . that is why, after having consecrated ourselves to His Sacred Heart, today we most solemnly dedicate and consecrate ourselves to you."

Was this desperate call on the Mother of all Mercies perhaps a secret premonition that something ominous was in the air, threatening to ruin him and all his hard work and institutions? On April 6, 1876, Comboni was in Rome, but very definitely not of his own will. Africa needed him the most, but he had been summoned to Rome to defend himself against accusations that could never be substantiated. It took seven long months during which he went through the "agonies of death." But finally the Sacred Congregation in its Plenary Session of November 27, 1876, recognized the complete innocence of Comboni. Pope Pius IX joyously confirmed the verdict the following December 10.

It is impossible to describe the joy of the intrepid Apostle. He wrote to Father Bricolo: "My institutions have come out untouched from this raging storm and will continue through the centuries to bring the light of the Gospel to Africa, stopping only at the threshold of Eternity."

And to Propaganda, he declared: "After so much suffering, I feel stronger than ever, by the grace of God. The conviction that crosses are the seal of the works of God comforts me and trusting in that Divine Heart which beats for Africa also, I feel more ready to sweat and suffer till my last breath, and ever ready to die for Jesus Christ and the salvation of Central Africa. . . . I am convinced that from this storm the African cause will gain. . . ." And that was all that counted for him.

But this good God Who never tries us more than we can take, Who "disturbs the joy of His children only to prepare for them another one more certain and great," this Lord of all goodness disposed that Comboni could receive during this same trying time the vows of "his" first sisters in Verona, October 15, 1876.

At last, he could have not only his priests and brothers, but also his sisters fighting side by side with him for the salvation of Africa. He called them "Mothers of the Africans." It really meant everything.

Bishop Canossa had provided the canonical erection of this second institute of Comboni in 1872, and the Founder procured a definite residence the very same year when he brought his first sisters from Montorio to Verona, to the very same place now occupied by their present Mother house. Again the main problem was to find a suitable person to be the superior of the small community.

A friend of Comboni suggested that he contact Maria Bollezzoli, a teacher in her forties, very active in her parish of St. Nazarus, in Verona, and a woman of brilliant mind and deeply good. Comboni got in touch with her as soon as possible, but she simply refused. Father Squaranti, director of Comboni's seminary, also tried but with the same result. When much later, Father Carcereri, Comboni's Vicar General, tried again, Miss Bollezzoli confessed that her spiritual director was in favor of her accepting, but she was still undecided. At that time, there lived in Verona a saintly religious well-known for her wisdom and practical good judgment. She was the superior of the Poor Clares. Miss Bollezzoli went to see her and as soon as she exposed her problem the good superior cut her short saying: "Accept! You will have the chance to do some good." After that, Bishop Canossa called her and finally she gave in. As she was leaving his residence, Canossa told her:

"Stop by Santa Maria—the convent of Comboni's sisters—and if God inspires you, stay." She went and she stayed. It was September 6, 1874.

The following December 8th, Feast of the Immaculate Conception, eight young ladies received the holy habit of the Mothers of the Africans. Bishop Canossa attended the closing ceremony in the evening and in his fatherly address he congratulated them and insisted that missionary life called for heroic virtues.

The aim of this institute was and is to co-operate with the missionary priests and brothers in the apostolate of Africa. The religious live a common life under rule and bind themselves by the three religious vows. Their title "Mothers of the Africans" is a continual reminder of their vocation. Their spirit has to be one of self-denial, zeal and love for God and His most unfortunate children. The institute is consecrated to the Sacred Heart of Jesus and put under the special protection of Mary Immaculate and of St. Joseph. Their habit is black, but they wear white in Africa. They wear on their breasts a small crucifix of white metal, held by a red twist which goes around their neck. The little cape has five buttons in front, also red, in remembrance of the five wounds of Jesus Crucified.

Comboni demanded from his missionary sisters the same heroic virtues he asked of his missionary priests and brothers. He used to tell them: "You are like shock troops . . . be prepared for a slow martyrdom. . . ." To those in charge of the formation of his missionaries he wrote: "Give me missionaries and sisters who are truly saints, I mean real ones because there is no room in Africa for fake-saints. We need generous and courageous souls who know how to suffer and die for Christ and for the Africans."

In July 1879, when presenting to Leo XIII five of his missionary sisters who were leaving for Africa, Comboni told the pope how he used to remind them, even when he wrote from Africa, that they were destined "to be butchered, to embrace the most painful privations and sacrifices, to undergo a slow martyrdom." Tears came into the eyes of Leo XIII while he congratulated them for their courage and exhorted them to persevere in their vocation. "The Mission of Central Africa," he added, "is immensely close to our heart!"

One day Comboni was asked if his sisters were classified as choir-sisters and lay-sisters. "No! No!" he answered promptly. "Among my daughters, there must be no difference between rich and poor."

In Africa he watched over them carefully, giving them practical advice and protecting them in every way. He used to recommend them to wear their crucifix so clearly visibly on their breast that everybody could see it when first looking at them and thus immediately recognized them as sisters. He wanted them to be cautiously reserved when going into public places and even in dealing with women.

Of course, Comboni was a man who used to practice what he preached. Knowing how necessary his sisters were in the African Apostolate, (particularly in the Mohammedan Sudan) he thought highly of them and loved them dearly. But in the meantime, he was always very reserved and grave with them. His saintly manners commanded deep reverence and veneration from all.

"He looked like an angel to us; just looking at him we felt obliged to be saints," testified one.

And others: "We had the greatest veneration for him."—"Upon observing him we were inspired to spiritualize our work."—"The servant of God was jovial with everybody.... The Africans, especially children, used to run after him, but his superior manners commanded respect particularly of women."

Comboni always defended and exalted the work of women in the missions and it was his example that inspired Father Arnold Jansen, the venerable founder of the Society of the Divine Word, to establish his own missionary sisters.

THE BERBER PLOT

In the preceding chapter we noted that just when Africa needed Comboni most he had to stay in Rome against his will for seven long months during which he went through the "agonies of death," while Propaganda Fide scrutinized his entire life. Certainly, all this arouses our legitimate curiosity, because a Sacred Congregation does not waste months for the sake of a joke and Comboni was not the kind of weakling to go through "agonies of death" over trifles.

Comboni's innocence was entirely vindicated, but apparently something ominous had been hanging over his head. What really was it? We honestly believe that plain truth, in the end, hurts less than mysterious silence. After all, there is nothing special about it in the sense that if Christ was denied and sold to be crucified by his best friends, why should we be surprised if something of the kind happened to one who most definitely wanted to be a real follower of Christ. ". . . In Berber they swore to destroy Comboni in order to take over the Vicariate and they *used any possible means* to succeed in it. . . ." Thus Father Squaranti wrote from Cairo (August 30, 1876) to Bishop Canossa. Father Squaranti, the rector of Comboni's Seminary in Verona, was sent there in order to find out the whole truth and prevent the

accusers of Comboni from carrying out their plans
while he was in Rome defending himself.

"The more I look at this mess," we quote again
from the same letter of Father Squaranti, "the more
it appears to me as a mystery of iniquity. It is but the
most bitter and insane hatred, the product of the
most crazy ambition which provoked all this terrible
war against the Pro-Vicar (Comboni)." We should
notice here that the one who was writing these extreme expressions was no other than the calm, self-
controlled, soft-speaking, prudent Father Squaranti.
Indeed, the unscrupulous enemies of Comboni used
"any means" to destroy him and the saintly rector
saw just that.

"They tried first," he went on, "to persuade the
missionaries, sisters included, to rebel against him.
This failing, they turned to accusations and horrible
calumnies."—As we have seen these were eventually
taken to Rome.—"But fearing that this too, would
not succeed, because sooner or later truth was going
to come out, they decided on a third way as the
most sure and efficacious means of demolishing
everything from the very foundations, that is, they
stopped all the donations and funds sent to the missions from Europe. They wrote to the benefactors,
both individuals and societies, that their money was
being very badly spent, or rather wasted; that the
mission was going to ruin and that bankruptcy was
inevitable. And, while writing that, they started
to build (without any necessity whatsoever and

against all economy) new houses in Cairo where so far 77,000 francs have been spent and they are not even half way through. The Pro-Vicar (Comboni), knowing the needs of the missionaries in the interior, had sent here 6,000 francs with orders to forward them immediately. On the contrary, Father Rolleri here in Cairo turns a deaf ear to it . . . with the intention, I think, of forcing those poor devils to run away in despair in order to avoid death by hunger. The correspondence between here and Berber is continuous; Father Stanislaus *vomits fire and flames* in every letter against the Pro-Vicar, against 'those stupids' of Verona who believe the tales of Comboni, and he threatens extermination if the Pro-Vicar will be confirmed as head of the Mission. That such are really the intentions and the actions of these gentlemen there is not the least doubt. What is currently happening is proved very clearly from the documents we have, and the way they act. Moreover, this is the opinion of people here in Cairo who know our troubles very well, such as Father Peter and Father Fabian, Franciscans; Father Simon, a Coptic priest, and others. . . . If we can save ourselves from this storm it is a true miracle and one more proof that the Lord wants this enterprise."

Thus wrote the calm, prudent, saintly Father Squaranti. But we might ask again: as the second of the three kinds of maneuvers against Comboni, Father Squaranti speaks of "accusations and horrible calumnies" without mentioning any.

It is easy however for us to shed some light on this matter through what was sent to and kept in Rome. Here are some of the "accusations and calumnies": because of Comboni's fault no sermons were preached in the missions; no catechism taught; conversions were few and the converts were being lost; money was being wasted in fancy buildings and vacations; Comboni was very worried . . . he was no longer head of the mission, he was dissatisfied with everybody . . . and therefore suspicions, frauds, injustices; the Kordofan mission was in disorder; the student seminarians wanted to go home as well as the sisters; El-Obeid Mission was in debt and in ruins; Khartoum was making a living by the sale of dates; the Seminary of Verona was loaded with debts; agreements were not being kept. Comboni was not saying Mass or the Divine Office; he had not gone to Confession for months and was accused of leading a blameful private life.—Here indeed the old Latin proverb comes to our mind: "He who proves too much proves nothing!" But Rome did not think so, and it was no wonder that it took seven long months to check one by one this catalogue of accusations.

The result was a triumph for Comboni. To someone of high rank who, because of the defeat, complained rather insistently to Cardinal Batolini, the Cardinal replied: "I advise you to stop it! Do you really want me to speak to you plainly? Here it is: *all* the Cardinals voted unanimously against your protegés; all unanimously condemned your friends and proclaimed that justice was on Comboni's side; all were against, not one voted in favor of his accusers. This is all: now go and do what you want!"

But who were these "enemies" of Comboni and what was their "precise aim" in this dangerous adventure?

The master-mind of the Berber plot was no less than the one whom Comboni had esteemed and loved so much as to make him his own Vicar General—Father Stanislaus. When the anti-clerical Italian government, following the pattern of the others in Europe, abolished all religious orders by the "Siccardi law," the young man—then twenty-eight years old—had asked to leave his order and join Comboni. It is certain that he had asked to leave his order *unconditionally and forever,* but all Bishop Canossa could obtain for him and his three companions (two of whom backed out almost immediately and no one else joined the other two in the next seven years) was a temporary permission to be renewed every five years. Faced with the problem of being obliged to go back some day under his old Superiors—who never gave him their blessing—the young man soon started to turn against Comboni, in the hope perhaps, of getting back into their graces. A very smart move indeed! From a very careful examination of all the documents, it appears that he was, in the end, for neither party, but was simply planning to build his own throne. "Therefore, he had first asked protection from Canossa and Comboni in order to free himself from his Superiors; then he leaned toward the latter in order to force the first to do what he wanted." (Grancelli)

In due time, Bishop Canossa warned Comboni against the ambitious young man, but Canossa himself confessed that Comboni did not believe him. On May 6, 1876, the Bishop had written a very long letter on the same subject to Propaganda Fide and among other things he said, "I have known for years the Rev. Father Stanislaus who is now a missionary in Berber; in fact, he was born in my diocese. He prides himself on having as his ancestors those Cimbri whom the famous Roman general Marius subjugated, but could not destroy. These people are stubborn, hard-headed, and tenacious beyond imagination. Father Stanislaus is every bit of this and his temperament is rather gloomy and closed. Now since going into Central Africa with Comboni he has tried everything, not only to implant his order there but to become the absolute, independent and sole master. I saw all of this a long time ago and I told Comboni, but he did not believe me. It is incredible how Comboni with all his talent, immense zeal for Central Africa and insuperable activity, can be so naive and credulous at times. He gave in to Father Stanislaus and let him have the missionary station of Berber, where I am told they don't do much for the salvation of souls. And now Father Stanislaus, taking advantage of two good but simple-minded missionary priests, Father Rolleri and Father Losi, has maliciously put to scrutiny the life of Comboni. From some minor defects of his (who is without them?) he has fabricated crimes and added horrible calumnies. He has pulled all strings possible to overthrow Comboni and deprive him of his Mission. I am sorry to say this, but it is a most certain fact of which I have all the proofs. And I know that somebody is already in Rome to pave the way to steal the whole Mission for themselves. They have entrenched themselves in Berber and they are trying to take over everything and to live off the altogether collossal fruits, sweats, fatigues, journeys, crosses, dangers, friendly relations and enterprises of Comboni! I feel better now in my conscience because I have told your Eminence everything and God knows that it is only with the desire of the salvation of souls." Thus testified Bishop Canossa.

After the letter of Father Squaranti that we quoted in part, the Bishop of Verona again wrote on November 6, 1876, to Cardinal Franchi, Prefect of Propaganda Fide, repeating the same charges. Among other things, he stated again very plainly that Father Stanislaus and companion were doing all they could to "take over the entire mission and kick out Comboni by any possible means—calumny not excluded." And the Bishop insisted that the above Father and companion must absolutely be removed "if we want to save the mission."

We can now understand how the calm, self-controlled Father Squaranti could have called the whole mess a "mystery of iniquity," the "product of the most insane ambition." Before closing this sad incident, however, we would like to disagree a little with Bishop Canossa on one point. The good bishop, who loved Comboni so much and fought so bravely for him, claimed in the first letter we quoted, that Comboni was "too credulous and even naive at times," (probably he meant gullible). We can understand how the bishop must have been disgusted with the whole business and particularly how from far away in Verona he could have seen the 'African story' from a different point of view than Comboni, who was in Africa and the head of the mission. We have to admit that Comboni was good-natured and could hardly doubt anyone, that he was particularly bitter against gossip which sows discord and division among confreres. But Comboni did always believe facts! Now he knew by heart the life of Father Stanislaus in Africa. It was hardly a year ago that Father Stanislaus had tried to pass the Asswan Falls of the river Nile, with two boats loaded with seventeen missionaries and 20,000 francs worth of merchandise. This was simply insane! And he should have known better because when he had tried before with a small boat and under more favorable circumstances he had failed. Naturally, he failed again. One of the boats broke, the sisters almost died with terror and a large amount of the precious merchan-

dise was lost. But he could have lost all the missionaries also! As if that was not enough, he continued
the journey by land, following a route that nobody
used any more because it was too long and difficult.
But *he was the boss!* The missionaries arrived in
Khartoum one month late and the cargo, upon which
the very life of the missions depended so much, five
months late. Comboni also knew well that the nice
sum of money—36,568,50 francs—of which Father
Stanislaus was so proud, was only a bluff! A cheap
bluff! Actually, only 26 francs could be attributed
to his personal work. History is history and mathe-
matics is not an opinion! And we could go on and
on! Yes Comboni had his defects and most certainly
he could not know everything, but he did know
plenty! But why, then, did he keep silent? Why did
he speak only when obliged to because he was accused in Rome? There is only one answer. Comboni
did have a weakness, a very great one, and this was
his immense love for Africa. To one of his missionaries, who had sided with his enemies in the Berber
plot, he once said: "My dear, write against me anything you want; write to Europe, to the Pope, to
anybody, but please, remain here and save my
Africans!"

This is Comboni. [1]

[1] For our purpose it is enough to barely touch this point. The
whole story has been properly treated by Gancelli, the first biographer
of Comboni, who dedicated to this question the entire second volume
of his work on Comboni.

SUCCESSOR OF THE APOSTLES

It was July 2, 1877, not even a year since Rome had solemnly declared the absolute innocence of Comboni. Now the same Rome, where Comboni had said: "Everything is done under the light of the Holy Spirit," spoke again nominating him Bishop and Vicar Apostolic.

Pius IX confirmed the nomination July 8.

The briefs of his nomination as Titular Bishop of Claudiopolis and Vicar Apostolic of Central Africa were published July 31. One of them reads: "Having lived in Africa for many years, you have given the most splendid proofs of your piety, your prudence, your counsel, your ardent desire and uncommon skill in promoting and propagating the Catholic religion."

Indeed that "Blessed Papal Rome, oasis of truth and justice," (the words are Comboni's) so careful in scrutinizing all his actions, was no less magnificent in rewarding his innocence and his merits. His elevation to the Episcopacy was the best proof of that.

On August 12, he was consecrated in the Church of Propaganda by the new Prefect Cardinal Franchi. We can easily imagine his emotion in receiving the fullness of the priesthood, the powers of

the Apostles, particularly when the consecrating
Cardinal gave him the Episcopal Cross to kiss and
to wear, the beloved, blessed cross that he loved so
much and that he so splendidly and bravely had
carried for so many years, at times all alone.

Pointing at this cross, one day he will say:
"This is a gift to prefer above all others because it
alone brings with it the honor of working for the
salvation of souls and of giving our own life for
them, after the example of Jesus Christ."

At his Episcopal consecration, he wanted the
superior of his seminary, Father Squaranti, present,
and Mother Bollezzoli for his sisters. That same day
Pius IX received him with the most tender affection.
He presented to him a pectoral cross with golden
chain, a precious ring and a silver crosier with the
pontifical emblem on it. In giving these gifts to him,
he said smiling: "This is really an outfit for a Cardinal more than for a missionary Bishop, but I
gladly give it to you."

In his coat of arms, the new bishop wanted a
big Africa flanked on either side by the blue ocean
bearing respectively a lion and crocodile in an ag-
gressive mood; high above them gleamed the hearts
of Jesus and Mary with the motto "In Hoc Vinces"—
with these Hearts you shall conquer!

Naturally, Bishop Comboni received for the
occasion many good wishes from far and near. One
letter came after a remarkable delay, but was probably the dearest of all. It was Bishop Massaia writ-

ing from Ethiopia. The saintly Bishop expressed all
his joy at the great news; he encouraged him to work
in his difficult mission without hope of human
recompense, and concluding he added: "How I desire to embrace you! which is impossible . . . but you
know that I love you, not for your handsome looks
but because of your great heart and for the love of
God that is burning in it."

Two days after his consecration, members of
his two institutes, the clergy and a huge crowd of
friends welcomed him at the railroad station at
Verona. But the first to greet him was his old father
who threw his arms around his Bishop son for a
prolonged embrace. Both were in tears.

Then an interminable procession of carriages
accompanied Bishop Comboni to the residence of
Bishop Canossa, then a Cardinal. And the last stop
was at the Institute for the African Missions. It is
impossible to describe the reception of his sons and
daughters! He was their founder, their father, their
only support after God. And here he was home after
long months of trepidation—tired, emaciated but
happy and made Bishop by the Pope. Some good
sisters thought perhaps this was the best time to
go crazy with joy. No, it was not a dream. Oh! how
grateful all were to the Sacred Heart and the dear
Madonna.

The celebration was climaxed with a carefully
prepared program in the afternoon. Around all the
walls of a beautifully decorated hall were inscrip-

tions and legends in many different languages—all the European ones, Arabic, of course, and many dialects of the tribes of Central Africa. When Bishop Comboni very obligingly went around the hall to read them, the Flemish seminarian Lotterman and a young Turk followed him, convinced that he certainly needed an interpreter at least for their two languages. The Flemish writing recalled the main events of Comboni's life, which he read and explained as if it were in his own native language. Lotterman could not believe his own ears. And the same happened for the Turkish writing. The young Turk, beside himself, exclaimed: "For heaven's sake, Your Excellency, how many languages do you know?" "Well," answered Comboni, "I know more or less all the languages spoken in Europe; naturally, I know Arabic very well and . . . oh, I don't recall how many African dialects."

At this point Father Manini, a professor in the diocesan seminary of Verona, could not resist playing a practical joke on the great linguist. (Comboni was famous for his sense of humor and love of harmless banter.) He presented him with a 'document' written indeed in a very strange language. Comboni read it over and over again, but at the end he confessed that 'that' language was unknown to him. Father Manini burst into a warm laugh. . . . It was the 'Hail Mary' in Latin, but all the words were written backwards!

The following day, the feast of the Assumption, he celebrated his first pontifical Mass in St. George Church with the same huge crowd of clergy and friends present. After the Mass one of the pastors of Verona delivered a sermon in Latin. That day, paper peddlers throughout town were yelling, "Bishop Comboni for five cents." He heard and commented smiling, "They sell me pretty cheap."

Limone, his native village, was anxiously awaiting its "illustrious son." When he arrived there on the evening of September 23, a big storm was in the air; nevertheless, two thick rows of people, one on each side of the street were stretched from the lake to the church. The small local band was playing its best pieces and there were all kinds of fireworks.

The following day the pontifical Mass was celebrated followed by many confirmations. In the evening under the "beautiful sky of Lombardy" the celebration reached the climax.

The next day, there were over 500 confirmations. At the banquet given in his honor there were 45 guests. When looking around, Bishop Comboni did not see his godfather and suspecting the reason why he was not invited, he stood up and asked aloud, "Where is my godfather? Just because he is poor, is he not supposed to be here?" They could stop Comboni from going after him only after he was assured that being too late then, they were going to invite him the following evening, which they did, and Bishop Comboni gave his dear old

godfather a new suit. People could not help thinking
how he was always the same Daniel, so wonderful
with the poor and the sick.

Soon after, while walking down the street, he
met a very poorly dressed old man. He stopped and
recognized his teacher of the first elementary grades.
He embraced him and walked along with him for
awhile. Upon leaving him he put a big donation in
his pocket.

On September 24, he said good-bye to his wonderful "Paesani," to the dear parish church, his
unforgettable mountains and deep blue Garda.
Everything was just beautiful, but the homesickness
awakened by the mysterious Nile and the constant
memory of his Africans suffering in slavery had a
much stronger appeal. "Africa or Death."

Back in Verona, he planned the European trip
that, due to his poor health, he had been advised
against taking soon after his consecration. Heedless
of personal well-being, he visited Austria, Germany,
France, Belgium. Everywhere he met old friends
who gave him most splendid receptions, with many
generous donations of which his missions were so
terribly in need.

In Brussels, he talked for two hours with King
Leopold II. The year before in the capital of Belgium, a conference had been held with the aim of
exploring and civilizing Africa, and abolishing
slavery. National committees were organized under
an international commission presided over by King

Leopold himself. Some of these committees had already contacted Comboni and now the king discussed further plans with the new Bishop. Among other things, he proposed a mission on the Congo River. Bishop Comboni asked for time and help.

Then he returned to Verona where the last days were passed in careful preparation for his near departure for Africa. The feast of St. Francis Xavier was solemnly celebrated in the church of St. Thomas the Apostle. At the Gospel, one of the departing missionaries, Father Piazza, delivered the sermon of farewell. Then they celebrated the feast of the Immaculate Conception and finally, on December 10, Cardinal Canossa bid farewell to the departing missionaries. Ten missionaries and five sisters were leaving with Bishop Comboni. Cardinal Canossa blessed the crucifixes and then put one around the neck of each missionary with his own hands. "Now, go and set all Africa on fire!" was his paternal remark.

At Verona's railroad station, Bishop Comboni and his father argued as to which of them was to receive the other's blessing first. In embracing his son, the old man said: "Oh, my God, I have only one son and I give him to You with all my heart; but even if I had many, I would consecrate all of them to You, for Your glory and the salvation of the souls You redeemed."

And the Bishop in turn replied: "Oh, my God, I leave my father, perhaps never to see him again . . .

but I would leave a hundred fathers, if that would be possible, to serve You, my heavenly Father, and to do Your will." He got on the train and wept.

In Rome, Pope Pius IX received him and his missionaries. Vaguely feeling, perhaps, that this was to be their last meeting on earth, Comboni had a prolonged look at the angelical Pius IX. He wanted to imprint on his mind forever the venerable features of the sweet pontiff who had always loved him so greatly, and who never doubted him even when all others had. He wished he could engrave in his heart his last encouraging words. A dear Pope, so good and so misunderstood and so persecuted! No wonder he had loved "His missionary" so tenderly; he was so much like him!

On the octave of the Immaculate Conception, in 1877, our missionaries sailed from Naples aboard the "Erebee." Everybody looked and smiled at the group of young missionaries flocking around the stout Bishop who seemed to be so much of a leader. All looked so happy. Yet many of them were never going to come back and they all knew it.

In Cairo, the Coptic and Greek Bishops, many European consuls and local authorities paid their respects to the new Vicar of Central Africa. Comboni paid a return visit to each one of them! The most important event of his stay in Cairo was a very long two hour meeting with the Kedive about the Sudan.

"I highly appreciate," he assured Comboni, "the information and advice you give me, because I know that coming from your venerable mouth, the suggestions are wise and true. I am very happy to see in Your Excellency such a great zeal and interest for the welfare of that country."

His son gave Comboni decrees for the governor general and all the authorities of the Sudan. How priceless these were for Comboni, above all in his determination to exterminate slavery!

Also on this occasion, Bishop Comboni met the famous explorer Henry Stanley who became a very good friend of his, and General Stone invited both to a party given in their honor. General Stone was president of the Egyptian Geographical Society. As a result, the secretary of the Society published an article highly praising Comboni, in which he most emphatically called him a real saint and a modern genius in Christianizing and civilizing the interior of Africa. Comboni could take anything—even praise—provided all served the cause of his African children. In commenting on these happenings, he wrote to Canon Mitterrutzner: ". . . And, at the end, all prayed for us. I have confidence in the most Sweet Hearts of Jesus and Mary that this time we will wage a real war against the devil and we will plant the cross in many places. . . ."

On June 28, 1878, the Bishop and his missionaries left for the interior by way of the Nile. At

Assiut, they heard of the death of Pope Pius IX. Comboni stopped for a solemn office and high Mass for the venerable Vicar of Christ and dearest Father.

At Asswan, he met Gordon, governor general of the Sudan, who was enroute to Cairo. The good friend confirmed what Comboni already suspected; a most devastating draught was hitting the Sudan in all its fury. He did his best to help Comboni get at least some of the necessary camels for the crossing of the desert from Korosco. When he arrived at Korosco, however, he found out that most of them had died from starvation.

The poor Bishop and his missionaries were determined not to turn back. Fortunately, Comboni could contact the great chief of the desert, an old friend of his, and by paying forbidden prices he was able to procure one-third of the camels he and his missionaries needed. And what camels! Some would certainly die along the way.

The crossing of the desert is always something unforgettable, but what it must have been in that year, 1878! Father Squaranti wrote: "Upon entering the desert, an awesome feeling of mysterious terror pervaded our hearts. Before us rose mountains of dark basalt thrown up by volcanos, perhaps during the formation of the earth, and burned for centuries by an implacable sun. . . . Along the road carcasses of camels were everywhere, skeletons and bones calcined by the infernal heat. . . . Everywhere, an unending sea of scorching sand where not a single blade of grass could ever sprout; where not a bird could be seen, nor cry of a beast be heard. . . . Above all, a frightening emptiness all around us gave us an idea of what a soul abandoned by God must be. . . . We suffered almost everything; the heat was at least 130° F. Because the little water in the containers had spoiled, we were devoured by a most horrible thirst, a thirst made even worse by the mirage that here and there came to torment us with crystal clear lakes, green isles and shady trees which kept running away from us as if in devilish mockery. . . ."

Our missionaries had to travel under these conditions about thirteen hours a day, at times over seventeen. It was impossible to say Mass. They used to say prayers together and at times they sang church hymns, particularly the "Ave Maris Stella" which must have sounded much more like a moan to the heavenly Mother of Mercy.

On March 26, they arrived at Berber where two of Comboni's missionaries were stationed. The Camillian Fathers had left the vicariate a few months before, recalled by their superiors to work in France. In this missionary station, the Bishop left the five sisters and with the others he proceeded to Khartoum by boat, April 4. On the 12th, he arrived in the capital of the Sudan. An immense crowd of people: Catholics, schismatics, Mohammedans, pagans, young and old, came out to meet their great Abuna, their great Father.

At last he was back with them. With him, hope returned to their hearts. They believed he could save them, or at least, that he was going to dare even the impossible to save them.

Comboni tried hard but, despite his efforts to smile at his tenderly loved children, tears filled his eyes. When his right hand instinctively went to press his heavy heart, he felt on his breast the cross the angelical Pius IX had given him. How heavy that cross was going to be from now on.

FAMINE

In the fall of 1877, a strange, sad thing happened in the vicariate of Central Africa; the rainy season never came.

The poor people had sowed their seeds as usual but nothing ever sprang up from the burnt soil. All grass and flowers had withered and died under the persistent penetrating sun. For people without any food reserve, it meant tragedy. Naturally, the little that was left climbed to fabulous prices—ten, fifteen, even twenty times the normal price. Wheat soon ran out. The usual food of the natives was durra and this went up even 100 times normal. In the Gebel-Nuba region, the shortage of food was not that desperate, but salt was impossible to get and the poor missionaries had to eat their already miserable meals completely without it.

"I witnessed with my own eyes," wrote Comboni, "the extreme miseries of so many places. Entire villages are almost destroyed. The few inhabitants left hardly stay alive by eating weeds, hay, and even the excrements of animals."

The Pro-Vicar Apostolic, as father of all, was everywhere trying to help as much as he could. Many times his missionaries told him he was too generous in his donations, but he never thought so.

His first duty, of course, was to take care of the institutions in the different missions which were composed not only of natives, but of young missionaries as well. More than a father, he was also a mother to them. The climate alone was murderous enough and in the present predicament with all the extra labors, they certainly could not go on without some decent food. But he knew that too often they did, and this was killing him. A sister in El-Obeid, for example, while in bed with a high fever, expressed her desire for a piece of wheatbread wet in water. Not even a little piece could be found in the whole town. In Khartoum, Comboni, as soon as he was told how bad things were in El-Obeid, bought twenty big sacks of wheat, over two hundred pounds each. He had it ground, but that was as far as he could go. He went all over Khartoum, even to the biggest merchants and the governor, but he was not able to find camels or men who could go as far as El-Obeid; either they had died or they were too weak for such a trip.

And yet the worst had not come for the missions of the interior. The torment from thirst is without comparison—it is even more unbearable than the pangs of hunger. El-Obeid, Malbes and Delen, being completely away from the reach of any river, got all their water from wells. Because of the unusually obstinate draught, little by little, many wells

went low and some ran completely dry. The latter
was true of the two big wells in the El-Obeid
mission.

Many Catholics and even some Mohammedans
came to the rescue of the missionaries with some of
their water, free of charge. But that was far from
being enough. The fathers were obliged to buy
much more at a very high price. It happened at
times that a missionary had to save the little wash
water he used in the morning in order to have something to quench his terrible thirst during the day.
For four months no laundry of any kind was possible.

"It is impossible to describe in words," Comboni wrote at this time, "the great privations suffered by our missionaries and lay-teachers. Boys
and girls keep calling on the fathers and sisters because they are burning with thirst, and when we
must turn them down they cry so loud it would
move a rock to compassion. . . . I would like to say
more, but I can't . . . most certainly God has written
in the Book of Life the heroic sacrifices suffered so
bravely by all our missionaries in this impossible
climate."

What the young missionary sisters did do is
amazing, almost incredible! Often at three in the
morning, the superior and one of the sisters would
leave the convent in El-Obeid with some containers,
a little bigger than gallon jars, and walk four or five
hours under the scorching sun to reach a well far
away. There they had to get in line and await their

turn, then almost put up a fight to get some muddy black water that was nauseating, pay five francs a gallon and start back to El-Obeid. Often they had to make the round trip in an afternoon to be back at the mission late at night.

At the model farm of Malbes, in a low spot, the missionaries, after sweating for weeks, succeeded at last in digging a new well. The water was by no means clear, but it was water. Of course, the news spread rapidly and guards had to be put up against the "water merchants" who stole water at night to sell in the daytime. Naturally, the water kept on being stolen, although the mission always had enough at least for bare necessities. In fact, many children from the El-Obeid mission were taken to Malbes. In Malbes, on the other hand, food was much more scarce; consequently they who ate breakfast could not eat lunch; and they who ate lunch could not afford to eat supper.

One evening they were notified that the water supplies at the El-Obeid mission had completely run out. At Malbes, almost all the missionaries were sick. A young sister therefore obtained permission to go to El-Obeid. They loaded a camel with two big containers of water and, with an African boy, the sister started her trip during the night. They were close to El-Obeid when the camel fell to the ground exhausted and no matter how hard they tried to get him up, it was to no avail. What to do next? To stay there in the open all night was not safe. There was danger from either the wild beasts or from water thieves. The heroic young nun left the boy to watch the water—blessed simplicity—while she went out into the pitch dark looking for help. And help this time was nothing less than two terrible Baggaras, by no means friendly people to the Christians. But that didn't matter on this occasion. They went back with the sister, made the camel rise and went with her and the boy to the mission of El-Obeid. It was midnight and the three travelers were dead tired, but not the Baggara tribesmen, who turned right back, and to the little sister who was trying to call her thanks after them, they simply answered: "Sure, Sister, anytime." History indeed repeats itself. Francis of Assisi and the wolf of Gubbio had met again that night in Central Africa.

To fill the chalice of the passion of the El-Obeid station to the brim, one more drop, the bitterest of all, was added. The altar wine ran out. Of course, no one could find transportation to or from Khartoum. The bishop managed to send them some in a small flat container by mail as often as the camel-courier was running. That way his beloved missionaries and children could have the Holy Sacrifice celebrated at least on Sundays and holy days.

Bishop Comboni's greatest consolation in all these trials was the heroism of his missionaries. To Cardinal Canossa he wrote, "I have to declare solemnly that none of our priests, brothers and sisters have ever failed in their courageous zeal in ministering to the needy of all kinds. They have stood bravely at their posts against the heavy attacks of so many destructive elements, trusting only in their Savior. And all that will mean even more if we don't forget that they have had fever most of the time and have been tortured day and night by unbearable mosquitoes. Everyone has been under the sweetest yoke of the cross, devoid of all human comforts, but sustained by the cross of Christ Himself, the infallible seal of the works of God."

The saintly bishop always spoke about the heroism of others, when his own great heart was carrying the weight of each and all of his missionaries' burdens. Of course, he did not have time to think of himself; only the others were working, only the others were suffering and saving souls. And to all that we should remember, another cross was added that was weighing only and entirely on his shoulders . . . the tremendous debt of the Vicariate.

On his return from Europe, he found it up to 45,000 francs, to which on account of the present calamities he was obliged to add 24,000 more. His creditors kept bothering him, but as he said, all in all they were pretty good, keeping the interest at a very moderate rate. We have to remember that in the Sudan the average interest rate was sixty per cent, but in some cases it went as high as two hundred and forty per cent.

Actually, the financial problems never did worry Comboni too much. His confidence in his heavenly Bursar was boundless, and in all truth, St. Joseph never failed him. In these most difficult times, he was writing to Propaganda: "Nothing like this had ever happened in this country . . . but in the beard of St. Joseph there are thousands and millions of francs. We have assaulted him so many times and so many are praying to him that I am most certain that the present financial problem of our missions will soon be changed. Time and troubles pass, we grow old, but St. Joseph is always young, always has a good heart and a fine brain. He always loves his Jesus and he is always interested in Jesus' glory, which in this case, is the conversion of all Central Africa."

And the great Bursar did provide again.

Bishop Comboni, however, whose glory was in being an apostle of Christ, and entirely sold to his cause, like Christ, had to ascend Mt. Calvary, and, the top was now very near.

DEATH LAND

Towards the end of July, 1878, after the driest spell in all Sudanese history, the sky was suddenly covered with black, heavy clouds. Then after an introduction of lightning and thunder of eschatological proportions, the most fantastic cloud bursts followed, off and on, for two consecutive months. The oldest of the natives could remember nothing like it. The White Nile and the Blue Nile soon overflowed their banks. Khartoum, situated at the confluence of the two rivers, would have been flooded in no time if the soldiers had not been kept busy day and night building a dam of dirt and sand all around it. Bishop Comboni had to spend a considerable amount of money and sacrifice hundreds of trees to protect the orchards of the mission. Between one storm and another, everybody was busy sowing as much seed as possible. Everyone thought that the long famine just suffered was going to be forgotten forever.

The torrential rains, little by little, however, disintegrated the fragile huts made of straw and mud leaving the poor natives exposed either to the rains or the burning sun for long weeks without protection of any kind. The results were disastrous. The most violent fever epidemic, probably a kind

193

of fulminant cholera, broke out all over the area.
People got sick and died within an hour. They fell
down in the streets and fields by the hundreds over
the beautifully abundant crops gathered in the
yards everywhere. Naturally nobody could take care
of the dead, so all those corpses, in advanced putri-
fication, rendered the air literally deadly.

Comboni wrote: "Having to go to Berber to
take five of our own sisters to Khartoum, I saw with
my own eyes what were once big villages, heavily
populated, now dead, silent, ghost towns. The very
few natives we could see here and there looked
more like walking corpses than anything else. Such
was, for example, the fate of the once-beautiful city
of Scendi, the old capital of the Nubia Kings, and
also of the once huge village of Temaniat . . . even
cattle had been practically all lost. We gave away
some food and alms to the few persons we met
alive, and the poor things could not find words
enough to thank us. . . ."

It has been calculated that in a region of the
Vicariate, as large as California, half of the population had died. In other parts even two thirds had
died. In many villages in a vast area south of Khartoum, not only all the people had died but all the
cattle as well.

All the marvelous harvests were wasted. Some
big merchants offered the government half of the
product if soldiers or workers of any kind were sent
to gather the crops. The government, so terribly

pressed financially, certainly could have used that thousand-dollar bargain, but was obliged to turn the offer down because there was hardly anyone to send. And that was not all.

In a letter to Cardinal Canossa at this time, Bishop Comboni reveals the heartbreaking effects of the epidemic on his own community! "... From that your Eminence can gather the terrible blow our finances got again. But who cares about money? ... Oh, how much suffering for all my missionaries and our African co-operators! ... And yet, what floods my spirit with unspeakable anguish, almost to the point of killing me, is the disaster caused by so many terrible sicknesses and deaths among them. The consequences for our mission, so permitted by the amiable and adorable Divine Providence, are irreparable. All that, however, through Divine Grace, has not succeeded in shaking our courage or in crushing the strength of our spirit. On the contrary, these supreme trials have reinvigorated our soul, and our trust is solely and entirely in the God of all mercies Who preceded us on the way of the cross and of martyrdom. So we are firm and resolute more than ever in this arduous, exacting, holy vocation of ours."

The deaths Comboni was referring to in his letter to Canossa occurred suddenly, from June on, during that unforgettable "Death Year" of 1878.

On June 13, Brother Birozzi passed away. On June 30, Father Genoud in fifteen minutes took

sick and expired. On July 15, Sister Gabriella died
and on August 30, Sister Arsenia.

Towards the end of September, when the torrential rains stopped, malignant fevers struck the
Khartoum Mission. All the Sisters were infected as
well as most of the children, many of whom died.
On October 22, the saintly Sister Enrichette, one of
the Sisters of the Apparition of St. Joseph still working with the Sisters of Comboni, passed away. On
November 4, Brother Mobardi died and two days
later Brother Iseppi.

"Everyday either a Sister, a Brother, catechists or catechumens are taken to their eternal
resting place by our Bishop or one of the Fathers
who are themselves ill with fever," wrote Father
Martini. "At dusk, after a day of exhausting fatigue,
and accompanied by some of our converts, I take the
last of the dead to the cemetery. I come back late
at night and I think that perhaps tomorrow somebody else will take me there."

As soon as some of the missionaries began to
feel better, Bishop Comboni sent them all by boat
to Gebel-Tajeb. It was a well-deserved vacation and
the saintly Bishop was hoping for their full recovery.
He forced the only priest who had not been hit yet
by the plague to go along with them. And he remained alone in Khartoum as bishop, pastor, bursar,
doctor, nurse, undertaker and father of all.

Before the horrible rains (the cause of the
present disaster) had started, Comboni had sent his

vicar general, the wonderful Father Anthony Squaranti, to Berber. He had been sick before and the Bishop wanted to save him from the deadly rainy season. The zealous Squaranti had written in October that he had recovered and felt stronger than ever before. But when he found out that the Bishop was all alone, without waiting for an answer to his letter, he left immediately for Khartoum by boat with Father Vanni. The boat was overcrowded. The trip lasted for fifteen long days. On the eleventh day, a very high fever attacked him again so violently that when he arrived in Khartoum and his Bishop tenderly embraced him, he was half dead. Comboni was terrified. He tried everything possible a father and mother could have done for their most beloved son. But all was in vain. Twelve days later, after receiving the Sacraments like a saint, and renewing again and again the offering of his life for the conversion of Central Africa, Father Squaranti died on November 16, 1878. It was evening and soon in the unique African sky a new star was lighting up. For the Bishop, however, it was a dark hour indeed.

Father Squaranti had been rector of Comboni's seminary in Verona for six years and had done a splendid job. Comboni had taken him to Africa hoping to have him some day as his coadjutor. His superior mind, his rare spirit of sacrifice and his passionate love for Africa made Comboni cherish the most promising plans for the future. But God wanted to realize the same plans in another manner. From now on the Bishop's "Consoling Angel" was *literally* to fulfill his heavenly role.

It might be said that the death of Squaranti was the death of Comboni. The unbeaten, indomitable giant, against whom hell had been throwing anything it had for years, was badly hit indeed that day for the first time. Physically, Comboni was never the same again. His sleeplessness, already bad, became worse. For five months, he had not been able to sleep one complete hour, day or night. Finally, on January 16, 1879, in the evening, coming back from a sick call, a murderous fever assailed him and forced him to bed at last.

The famed explorer Dr. Matteucci at this particular time wrote to Europe from Ethiopia a long, moving letter describing the horrors of the Sudan and imploring help, in most desperate words, for Comboni and his missions. ". . . Almost everything and everybody has been lost . . . and now there are no more than two or three heroes with their splendid leader Comboni, left only to weep over ruins. . . ."

When the tragedy was close to the climax, some missionaries could resist no longer and went back to Europe. The Superior General of the Sisters of the Apparition of St. Joseph also thought of recalling from the missions the sisters she still had there.

These were the last drops which filled to the brim the Chalice of the bitter passion of the martyred Bishop.

And yet during all this agony not a word from him, either written or spoken, which might give even vaguely a hint of regret or surrender. "We will face without fear. . . even death for the salvation of these souls. . . ."

Terms like "compromise" or "surrender" did not even exist in Comboni's vocabulary.

Always and unconditionally: "Africa or Death!"

TERRIBLE TOOTH ACHE

The great dream of Comboni had always been to reach the Great Lakes at the Equator where the natives were still immune to the poison of Mohammedanism and free from the curse of slavery. In the beginning of 1878 the apostolic delegate of Egypt had given him a letter from Propaganda in which Cardinal Franchi inquired about the plans of the king of Belgium for the Congo, and what had been done about it up to that time. Comboni answered on January 19th: "So far only a small expedition of four men has left Belgium and is now close to Lake Tanganyika . . . I know the leader, Mr. Marno from Vienna. . . I will give a full report later regarding the King's plans which we discussed together for over two hours . . . I will say, in general, that some European governments, after useless efforts to civilize Central Africa without God, will bow before the power and sacrifices of the Catholic Church, the only one able to bring to those unfortunate people the long-lasting benefits of the Christian civilization . . . . I have also had long conferences with the great explorer Stanley who is just back from Equatoria and Congo. . . . I will write you about many more interesting things. . . . To the invitation of the King

of Belgium I answered that first I must establish the
missions at the Equatorial lakes before thinking of
the Congo. . . . "

As soon as Governor General Gordon was back
from Cairo, Comboni went to see him about the
expedition to the Equator. The kind Gordon answered: "Right now I cannot help you. I said the
same to four Anglican missionaries who are in Suakim and plan to reach Lake Nyanza. I told them
that, when I can, I will do not a single inch more
for them than for you who have been in the Sudan
for many years. . . ."

A few days later, to the great surprise and joy
of Comboni, Captain Gessi came to see him with
good news from General Gordon. "Tell Bishop Comboni that I want to help and the expedition will be
at my expense as far as the transportation of the
missionaries and their luggage is concerned. He will
have only to take care of the food." Captain Gessi
then explained the plans of Gordon: to take the
missionaries by steamboat from Khartoum to Lado;
then to cover the 120 miles to Lado-Dufilé by foot
with all the necessary help; from Dufilé to continue
by steamboat on to Magungo and Lake Albert; then
by canoe to reach Lake Victoria and Lake Nyanza.
Comboni was beside himself with joy. "So I wrote to
his Excellency the Governor a nice letter in English
thanking him most warmly and assuring him that
I was going to get busy immediately. . . ."

The date of the expedition was set for the fall of 1878 which, as we know, turned out to be the "Death Year." So, for the time being, nothing could be done.

Moreover, something else had happened. In the beginning of the same year, Bishop Lavigerie of Algiers had offered his missionaries to Pius IX for the Equatorial Africa.

Pius IX had died and Leo XIII only four days after his election signed the decree of approval. When Comboni was notified that the land of his dreams was cut off from his territory, he could not hide a sense of deep sadness. He humbly asked Propaganda Fide if it were at all possible to give to Bishop Lavigerie only the territories south of Lake Nyanza, but he promptly added: "At any rate I declare in all sincerity that I am ready to do whatever the Holy See wishes me to do. . . . Even to give up Khartoum and Kordofan and everything else. . . . The Holy See is the only master and abitrator of all."

One year later he was happy to write to Cardinal Simeoni, the new prefect of Propaganda, that he had warmly recommended the missionaries of Algiers to his good friend Emin Bey, governor of Equatoria, and that through consul Hansal he knew they had been well received by King Mtesa.

Meanwhile, during the calamity of the famine and plague, God had sent to his faithful servant *some* consolations. Many, many baptisms were administered to the dying everywhere. In Khartoum sixteen converts were solemnly baptized; about a dozen at Gebel-Nuba and Berber and a few also at Gedaref. The amazing thing was that many of these were converted from Islamism and gave proof of great courage in the practice of their faith.

A very great comfort also to the heart of the suffering Bishop was the tremendous spirit of sacrifice shown by all his beloved daughters, the heroic "Mothers of the Africans" whose institute he had founded just few years before. The first trial of their spiritual formation had yielded the most superb results. Whoever had come in contact with the young sisters had but the deepest admiration and veneration for "those little angels from heaven." General Gordon never ceased asking the Bishop for some of them for the military hospitals of Fascioda and Lado.

These were real consolations. But in spite of them, when the spring of 1879 came, Comboni's poor health did not show much sign of improvement; he could not sleep, he could not eat. The English doctor of the governor insisted very strongly on treatments of thermal baths and vacation in Italy.

Finally, Comboni gave in, although for rather different reasons. He had an immense desire lately to talk to Cardinal Simeoni, Prefect of Propaganda, concerning his missions of Central Africa. He was also still hoping to persuade the Superior General of the Apparition to keep some of her sisters in Africa a little longer. But the Number One reason for this trip was that Comboni's seminary in Verona, after the saintly Father Squaranti had left, did not have as a rector a man really capable of such a difficult and delicate task. This was a bad situation, especially since the salvation of Comboni's Africans depended on that seminary. So he left for Italy, arriving in May, 1879.

His loved ones, his friends, all those who had seen him two years before could hardly recognize him. He was only forty-eight and yet he looked like an old man. His beard was growing gray, his shoulders had lost their majestic erectness, his face gave evident signs of long and protracted suffering. Only his love for Africa had not diminished and his boundless trust in God was still the same. On January 2nd of that year he had written from Khartoum to Cardinal Simeoni: "I drop your Eminence only a few lines because I am broken with fever, tribulations, fatigue, and bitter anguish is in my heart ... but, though broken physically, my spirit, by the grace of the Heart of Jesus, is still strong and firm. I am determined now, as I have always been since 1849, to suffer anything and give my life a thousand times for the redemption of Central Africa."

In Verona he immediately got busy, looking for a rector for his seminary. The Superior General of the Society of Jesus turned him down again for lack of personnel. On August 3rd, he wrote to Cardinal Canossa: "The thought of my seminary does not give me any rest. I appreciate your suggestion to call on the Stigmatine Fathers so they may take over at least until the Jesuits will be able to come. With tears in my eyes I beg your Eminence to come to my help. God will bless you and your diocese of Verona.... There are good subjects in both our institutes ... I want to make true Apostles out of them. I don't care what others might say; as for me, in this most important affair, I am Jesuit and Stigmatine to the finger tips."

Father Joseph Sembianti was the Stigmatine assigned to his seminary. Comboni was very happy over the appointment and wrote to the rector-elect: "I don't have words enough to thank Jesus, Mary and Joseph for the signal favor given to our dear Africans in choosing your wonderful institute to cooperate with us in the work of their salvation with efficacy and determination....I shall never be able to thank as I would like to the exquisite charity of your very Reverend Superior General...."

From now on, Comboni will always stay very close to Father Sembianti giving him all the advice he needs in this "most important job of all, for the salvation of Africa."

We have over forty letters written by him to the new rector. Some of them are very long, all in a plain style, confidential, all showing a terrific love for God and Africa. In one he says: "Pray that we may launch an all-out war on the devil in Africa, break his horns, ruin him, destroy him and make the kingdom of Christ triumph . . . and pray for me also in a special manner, because I am the most isolated Bishop in the world. . . ."

From the correspondence of Father Sembianti in turn we gather that he was no lion! The missionary Bishop keeps on encouraging him, trying to infuse in him some of his sound optimism. Good psychologist that he is, he even goes so far as to put himself up as an example on one occasion: "In all the works of God we will always have great difficulties because we have the devil against us. . . . What could I have done if I had been afraid of the devil who has his allies among the bad and among the good as well? . . . The Holy See would not have been able to implant the African Mission. Let them talk there in Verona, but the Holy Father and many very brave missionary bishops are all convinced that it was due to the unshakable determination of that cheap cobbled and big sinner Comboni, backed by all the fervent prayers of the world and the heroism of his missionaries. Comboni is good for nothing, and yet that most difficult mission of his still stands. . . . So, my dear Father, go on with courage, don't be afraid. With the Heart of Jesus, and Our Lady of the Sacred Heart, our good Bursar Joe, the advice of your venerable Superior General and under the mantle of the Cardinal Bishop of Verona we will succeed in everything. I am not afraid of the whole universe. The interests of Jesus and the Church are at stake and we will not become useless foundation-stones for the building of the African Church."

Another time he wrote to him: "Think of all the merits you will gain, think of the army of apostles, of virgins, of Africans who will accompany you triumphantly into heaven. . . ."

Comboni was by nature and by grace vigorous, forceful, and he wanted his missionaries to be the same. How cleverly he knew how to mix bitter with sweet to attain his aim. Once Father Sembianti excused himself for something, and Comboni replied: "You don't have to excuse yourself. I know that people just like to talk and I believe you, not them. But the fact that you are so anxious to excuse yourself proves that in matters of sound and proved virtue, of true, deep humility and desire to carry the cross and become 'Anathema' like the Apostle, you are still a child and far away from a real triumph over self. Forgive me, dear Father, if I dare to teach you about the spiritual life, when I am much poorer than you in all these virtues and have a cartload of defects, whereas you are like an angel. But I am the head of this institution, which being destined for the most difficult apostolate, has to make saints, and you are the first instrument God wanted to make these saints. . . . So you have to learn little by little very deeply, the 'Anathema' of the human spirit to be able to make holy apostles. If I speak to you this plainly, it is because I want you to do the same with me, for our correction and confusion . . . and for the salvation of the poor Africans, who are the most abandoned souls of the world."

In September, 1880, three months before his return to Africa, Comboni was notified by Rome of its final decision to cut off from his vicariate all the regions of the Equatorial lakes. With that the entire Equatoria province was lost and even Gondokoro and Holy Cross where he had worked for the first time and where his heroic young companions had died and were buried. All of Comboni's territory was now exclusively under Islamic influence.

Answering the communication of Propaganda Fide, the poor Bishop simply said: "This is a terrible toothache which will last as long as I live or until the Sacred Congregation will decide otherwise."

The Equatorial lakes remained his great dream and he always kept himself in contact with friends and pashas for a possible return there.

But it was written in heaven that the "terrible toothache" was going to be with him to the very last breath. Not until 1894 would Cardinal Ledokowski, the new Prefect of Propaganda give back to Comboni's sons all of Equatoria and north Uganda, because in these territories missions had failed to be established as planned in 1880.

GOODBYE, LIMONE

Bishop Comboni was now ready to go back "home" to Africa, his country by adoption. His one year and a half stay in Italy had been very profitable. He had been able to take care of quite a bit of important business and above all, his beloved seminary. Also his health had improved considerably, although he had suffered some bitter attacks of fever even at home.

He also had the chance to keep the promise made to his "Paesani" of Limone during the great celebrations for his episcopal consecration. "I will be back to consecrate our parish church," and a few months after his return to Italy in October, 1879, he had done just that. At the end of the ceremony, he looked radiant. That dear old church meant so much to him. There he had given Holy Communion for the last time to his mother on that far-away morning during the summer of 1857, before her final consent and blessing on his missionary vocation.

But the most moving memory of all was the one which took him back to his childhood. How many times he had come there to talk to his God and to receive Him so lovingly! How many times he had knelt at the altar of the Mediatrix of all Graces and never tired of looking at her beautiful eyes and finally, had gone away convinced that she had smiled at him as an assurance of her maternal love. The Masses he used to serve, the vespers he used to sing, his Pastor's sermons, those unforgettable catechism contests. How good the Lord had been to him! How invaluable the grace of such an intense and rich parish life! Even the smell of that blessed air seemed different, unique. Coming out the door he had to turn back to look at it once more, his eyes in tears. Too bad he had to go and this time for good.

Just before crossing the unforgettable blue Garda, for the last time, his cousin was sure to tell him: "Your Excellency, when you get older I hope you retire in Rome or . . . elsewhere."

"My dear," he answered excitedly: "The gate of heaven can also be found by dying in Africa."

He could not resist any longer the mysterious attraction of his dear African children, of his institutions, of his missionaries whom he esteemed and loved so much.

He left Verona on November 23, 1880, and on the 27th, sailed from Naples for Alexandria, Egypt. At Cairo the Kedive received him splendidly and generously as ever, favoring him with many concessions for his missions. So did the pashas.

By Christmas Day he blessed the cornerstone of a new church dedicated to the Sacred Heart, to be erected between the two buildings of the boys and the girls in old Cairo. On December 31st with some of his missionaries, he sailed from the Suez for Suakim on the Red Sea, where they arrived January 5th.

On January 10th, with forty camels, they began the crossing of the Korosco desert. From the Red Sea the crossing was much easier and shorter, although the water, nauseating and of an undefinable color, remained their number one problem. To fool their palates and their eyes they drank it mixed with a little coffee in small tin cans. The supply running out, they had to refill at the very same puddles where the animals would drink. They traveled from ten to twelve hours a day and the Bishop, though very tired himself, used to entertain and encourage all, particularly the young ones. Like a good father he would ask in the morning and in the evening how each one felt. Having noticed one day that the camel on which a young sister was riding was acting rather strangely, he started to ride very close to her and fortunately so for the little sister. The animal all of a sudden threw its light rider up in the air, but Comboni was ready and she landed safe on his own camel right in his arms.

After twelve days they reached Berber where the comfortable mission residence offered them a nice rest. A pleasant surprise waited there for Bishop Comboni: a steamer was anchored on the Nile for him and his missionaries. The kind Kedive from

Cairo had telegraphed General Gordon in Khartoum to treat their good friend well, the venerable head of the Catholic Church in the Sudan.

After only twenty-nine days, they docked at Khartoum, joyfully acclaimed by the fathers, the sisters, the children of the schools and many, many people.

The trip had been the fastest ever and seemed like a miracle. From Cairo to Khartoum it used to take at least three months, although today, of course, it is only a short pleasure excursion by air. All this gives some idea of the tremendous difficulties those heroic pioneers had to overcome even only in this one point of traveling. "They were dead before arriving," it has been said, and the statement is not far exaggerated. This also proves to some extent how guilty of ridiculous ignorance the modern writer is who attributes the high death rate of those heroes only to their complete lack of "know-how!"

On the day following the arrival of the missionaries, a solemn "Te Deum" was sung in church. Soon after, Bishop Comboni came out to meet the huge crowd. He shook hands and talked to everyone, from the governor down to the last African who remained to greet him.

Father Pimazzoni wrote to Verona of this occasion: "Our dear Father really can be big with the big, and small with the small, and if they are natives he betrays his predilection for them. He consoles them, he advises them and assists them in whatever they ask. Such conduct on the part of our Bishop is a continuous lesson for us. He teaches us how to be humble and charitable with anyone."

Comboni was back on time to assist Gessi Pasha then very sick in Khartoum. The hero of the Bahr-El-Ghazal got well again and attributed his recovery to the mission, particularly to the sisters who were at his bedside day and night.

Gessi and General Gordon were the only two men in authority who understood Comboni and shared his own ideals. Like him they sincerely wanted the real good of the Africans; like him they were determined to fight slavery to the end. Both Gordon and Gessi—the one English, the other Italian—besides being in love with Africa also had so much else in common. "Both were at their best in irregular guerilla warfare, for by nature they remained cool and steady in the most bizarre and dangerous of circumstances," wrote Allen Moorehead in his *White Nile!* [1] "They were men of the commando type and they complemented one another very well: where Gordon was sensitive, solitary, and ascetic, Gessi was warm-hearted and gregarious and both were impulsively brave. They were equally prone to violent outbursts of anger, but that too may have been a bond, for it cleared

[1] Quoted with permission of Harper and Row Inc. Publishers.

their differences like a sudden thunder-storm, and always in a crisis they were loyal."

Comboni wrote of Gordon who was an Anglican: "He reads the Bible for three hours every day, lives without women like a monk, and prays very much. . . . He believes that the Catholic Missions do more good than the Anglicans and all the others. . . ."

Romolo Gessi was the first man able to wipe out slavery from Western Sudan. In the summer of 1878, he attacked the slavery-boss Suleiman with a contingent of troops in the Bahr-El-Ghazal province; he routed him and, expert in guerilla warfare that he was, kept after him persistently, not giving him a moment to rest or hide or to reorganize his bandits. In the end he ambushed him and killed him together with all his chief assassins.

"Ten thousand slaves were released," writes Allen Moorehead. "It was a fast and brilliant operation, the first of the great guerilla battles in the Sudan and the only one in which a European commander showed any real understanding of the nature of the war against the Arabs. Its effects were remarkable. For the first time in twenty-five years, the western Sudan was freed from the tyranny of the Zobeir and his family and, for the moment at least, the wholesale traffic of slaves was checked."

Writing to Father Sembianti, Comboni declares: "Gessi is a true hero. He loves priests and sisters, but has never had much chance to practice his religion. He wanted a letter for you from me because he wishes to come to see you and thank the sisters again in Verona."

Gessi had loaned our Bishop 20,000 francs without interest or return date. He also asked him to establish the Catholic Missions in the Bahr-El-Ghazal at his own expense, any time he had missionaries available.

March 15, 1881 was Comboni's birthday and practically all Khartoum was around him to celebrate. The local authorities and the European consuls came to present their wishes and stayed for the dinner in his honor. General Gordon had the military band present also.

Comboni wrote: "On the fifteenth of this month I was fifty years old. My God, we grow old. and the trials and crosses seem to increase. But since these crosses come from God, so do I hope in His divine help. O Crux, ave spes unica."

And to make the feast complete he "put the bite" on St. Joseph for 60,000 francs to be paid by August. To prove that he meant business, he invited all the guests to sign the paper for the deal. Some were surprised, some amused, but all signed it except one who judged the thing a kind of tempting of God. Of course, this particular person changed his mind when the money came in the full amount and at the right time!

The Bishop was very eager to visit the missions in the Kordofan and the governor provided a steamer for him as far as Tura-El-Kadra. When he arrived there, he found swift dromedaries ready for him, kindness of General Gordon. In only ten days (March 26th-April 5th) he was at El-Obeid.

It was the first time he had visited there as a Bishop, and a missionary wrote: "It was a real feast, a universal joy not only for the Catholics, but for Mohammedans and pagans as well. Our Bishop was really all to all with his kind and friendly ways, his big heart embracing everyone, loving everyone and winning over the love and esteem of all. . . . There were in El-Obeid three fathers, two brothers and four sisters, all doing wonders for the salvation of souls. . . ."

The schools were crowded with children, over 100 of them were boarding students, the mission taking care of all the expenses. The Bishop was happy to bless the new church built the year before. It was about one hundred feet long and forty feet wide. Two rows of eight columns demarcated the nave from the two flanking aisles. The windows were big and in color. The building was an authentic marvel for El-Obeid where, except for the governor's house, everything else was just plain huts made out of mud and straw. The faithful contributed with their small donations, but almost everything was done by the missionaries themselves. Three thousand lires were spent just for the water used to mix the adobes. In the beautiful church Bishop Comboni celebrated his pontifical Mass on Easter Day.

Father Bouchard also sent good news from Khartoum. "All the Christians able to walk were here Easter morning: we did not know where to put them. But the most consoling thing of all has been the number of Holy Communions. All the Africans of the mission received Jesus. My poor heart was flooded with joy."

After Easter, the missionary Bishop set forth on his expedition to Gebel-Nuba. He visited Malbes, the model-farm village first, and at the end of May he left for Delen with Father Bonomi, Father Marzano, two sisters, and a few pupils of the mission. All traveled by camel except the Bishop who had to accept the personal horse of Governor Said.

As we know already, the aim of this trip, besides visiting Delen, was to find a place in the interior for a new mission, but above all to pass one by one all the mountains and valleys, to be able to make a detailed report about the disasters caused by the slave traders and to suggest the proper means to the governor general for getting rid of that abominable shame of mankind.

This news had leaked out and all the slave traders were in terror. Comboni shared the fatigues and discomforts of all this traveling with his missionaries. The food was less than poor and often consisted only of a little raw pulp without salt prepared by the natives.

"He edified us all," wrote Father Losi, "with his wonderful acceptance of all kinds of hardships from the people and from the elements; he was always extremely kind in comforting and pleasing the sisters. . . . He wanted to see all the mountains around, and over-worked himself like a soldier, under the most trying conditions of weather and lodging."

On July 8th he was back in El-Obeid, but he was exhausted. The missionaries did everything possible to make him regain his strength, but to no avail. He was not able to eat; neither could he sleep at night. On July 21st, the feast of St. Daniel, all the personnel of the mission, to prove him their most loving affection, organized a magnificent celebration. To make the occasion complete and more according to the Bishop's taste, they purposely kept for that day the conferring of the sacrament of Baptism to a few adults and of the sacrament of Confirmation to some fifty neophytes. Practically all the Catholics of the mission received Holy Communion for him. . . .

On leaving for Khartoum and when saying good-bye to each one of his wonderful missionaries of El-Obeid, he could not hide behind his usual smile a sense of painful sadness. "Pray for me very, very much," he begged. "I will never come back again."

"IT IS CONSUMMATED"

The trip El-Obeid-Khartoum turned out to be disastrous. A terrible equatorial storm caught our missionaries on their way at night. They were forced to stop under the torrential rain and the Bishop had to lie down in the water. Actually his little mattress was under water.

Fortunately, the good Governor General Rauf had a small steamer ready for him at the Nile so that he could reach Khartoum in one day with his missionaries.

At the capital all were hoping for his speedy recovery, but his health kept getting worse instead. Attacks of fever became more frequent; he could hardly force himself to eat anything and the insomnia he had suffered for years now reached an alarming point—he was not able to rest one hour out of forty-eight.

His long "way of the Cross" had come to an end and the time for his last agony on the cross was at hand. Not long after his arrival in Khartoum the martyred Bishop was told of a hideous calumny of the lowest type against him which had reached Verona. . . . This was really plenty, although Comboni never had been very concerned about himself. However, when someone told him that either by

ignorance or diabolical malice the thing had been
made known even to his old father, he became desolate. He wrote a long letter to Father Sembianti on
August 13, 1881 in which he says, among other
things: "... my sorrow is extreme. Let them inveigh
against me, let them renounce me to the Pope ...
but to disturb and torture a holy old man ... this
is too much! ... In the most adorable wounds of
Jesus I recommend to you my father, Louis Comboni. ..."

"How dear the mission of Central Africa and
its venerable head must be to God if they are so
calumniated and persecuted ...." wrote Father
Bouchard, the superior of Khartoum. And he added:
"But any honest man is obligated to give testimony
to the truth and bow before merit and virtue."

As for himself, Comboni was happy when everything was brought to the Holy See. "At Rome," he
wrote, "they judge in the light of the Holy Spirit. ...
I am really happy... now more than ever I am at
peace and certain that innocence, justice, and truth
will triumph."

But the third nail, as it were, that came to fasten
and keep him tight to the cross until his last breath
was sickness and death again among his beloved
missionaries. He loved them so much that anything
happening to them had severe repercussions on his
own fatherly heart. And yet in spite of all, he kept

working. His correspondence in the last months of his life reached an all-high. His letters were not only many but very long.

On September 20th, he wrote to the Girellis: The other day we celebrated the Office and Requiem Mass for Father Moron, a very pious young man from Poland whom I had ordained to the Priesthood. Before the catafalque was taken away, I received from El-Obeid the news of the death of another of our missionaries—Father Dubale, an African whom I ransomed when he was a boy and had sent to study in Rome. Yesterday we celebrated the Office and a Requiem Mass for him, and do you believe it, that right after, a note was given to me from Malbes of the death of Sister Colpo? . . . She died like a little heroine and saint, as happy as a bride on the day of her wedding. . . . What shall I do? This morning after the Requiem Mass for our dear Sister, I gave orders not to move the catafalque because I expect other kisses of this kind from our loving Jesus who showed, so to speak, more genius in inventing the cross than creating the heavens. . . ."

To his apostle suffering on the cross, God gave a last consolation. On October 2nd, he administered fourteen Baptisms to adults, ex-pagans and Mohammedans. Among them was an old Dinka, whom he called John Chrysostom, after his dearest canon Mitterrutzner, and a young lady, daughter of the ex-commander in chief of the troops of the Gordofan and Darfur. She had begged her mother for five years and finally, her prayers had been answered. However, this bit of consolation was only a short interlude. On October 3rd, at 7 in the morning, Paul Scandi died. He had taken sick one week before and had told his Bishop that he felt fortunate if God were going to call him. After the Extreme Unction and papal blessing he exclaimed: "Now I am really happy!"

The preceding night the Bishop had assisted the theology student Pimazzoni who had become very seriously ill. The same day, October 3rd, Father Fraccaro took sick and soon he was on the critical list. Comboni had brought him from El-Obeid because he was planning to make him his Vicar General. How similar was Father Fraccaro's case to Father Squaranti's in 1877! With the big difference that what Father Squaranti almost did, Father Fraccaro was going to do—cause Comboni's death.

With supreme effort, Comboni tried to hide his own unspeakable suffering, both physical and moral, continuing to be the consoling angel to his sad and discouraged missionaries. But his super-human effort was not going to last much longer; his Calvary-time was running out. On the night of October 4th, while visiting his dear sick around the house with Father Dichtl, he stopped at a certain point and said with a smile: "Don't you see how sweet the cross is?"

The following morning he was running a fever and unable to say Mass even in his own room as he had been doing lately. The fever seemed to have left him by October 8th. The following day at noon, Father Fraccaro died a saintly death. The Bishop collapsed in tears. He was never to be himself again.

"His words were as always consoling and all resigned to God's will, but they no longer had that magic power so unique to him," wrote young Pimazzoni. "All that suffering had robbed our beloved Bishop of some special qualities so typically and exclusively his . . . . So everything was sadness and sorrow around us. . . ." and he added very significantly: ". . . It was painful even to think!"

That evening, October 9th, Bishop Comboni talked for a long time about his crosses, his dear missionaries, his friends and benefactors, his dear old father in Limone, his Africans, all his missions— it was his last night here on earth.

On the morning of the 10th he somehow dragged himself to see the sisters. He knew that their spirits were very, very low, yet so faithful to the last to his rule of forgetting himself to serve the others, and staggering in a sweat, he managed to reach the convent, while the fathers were carrying Father Fraccaro to the cemetery. When they came back he was in bed, terribly grieved but resigned to the loss of dearest Fraccaro. Everybody could see how much he was suffering and yet he kept consoling them, urging them to have so much

courage now and "particularly in the future." Overcome with emotion, he repeated, "particularly in
the future."

Perhaps God had revealed to him what was in
store for the Sudan in the very near future—the
bloody Madhi revolution which threatened to wipe
out all his flourishing missions, fecundated by so
many sacrifices and consecrated by the tombs of
some hundred missionaries.

Then very humbly he asked pardon of all present and absent and repeated again and again almost in tears: "I forgive everybody!" A couple of
hours before noon he asked for the sacraments: "I
feel bad, we don't know what might happen particularly here." With ardent fervor he received the
sacrament of Penance, and right after, Holy Communion. Very soon the usual signs of the "black
fever" appeared. He lost consciousness for two
hours. When he regained consciousness, convulsions
kept impeding his speech.

"I will never forget the last hours of our beloved
Father and how wonderful he was," wrote young
Pimazzoni. "Entirely abandoned into God's hands,
even in his delirium he kept his usual pleasant amia-
bility which made him so dear and respected even
to his enemies. At times, opening his eyes and
looking at his sons and daughters standing desolate
around his bed, tears would appear in his eyes: how
much he loved us; how sorry he was to leave us and
his Africa. But he soon plunged himself into com-

munion with God repeating to his beloved Lord burning acts of love, of resignation to His will, of confidence, of sorrow."

At five in the afternoon he seemed to feel better; his mind became very clear and the great passion of his whole life, Africa, took over as a dominating thought. Father Dichtl was at his bedside. The venerable Bishop, taking the hand of the young priest in his own, asked him to renew the missionary oath to spend all his life for Africa. All the missionaries felt relieved and went to church to pray before the Blessed Sacrament, solemnly exposed all day, and to join the faithful in thanksgiving because their beloved Father had been given back to them.

But it was not so. "God did not listen to our prayers," wrote young Pimazzoni, "because his crown of merits was perfected by the last sufferings and He could not wait to reward him with the eternal glory. . . . After a while he became delirious again, the fever mounted and at eight in the evening he was in severe convulsions. Oh, how greatly the soul of our founder had merited in such a painful state. Being conscious, he was able to understand all the pleas of his sons and daughters; he read in their eyes their terrible sorrow but could not talk. Only through great effort he could pronounce rather intelligibly with burning ardor, "My Jesus, mercy." Two of the fathers gave him Extreme Unction and the papal blessing. He followed each single detail (of the sacrament) with visible devotion. Then Father Bouchard bending slightly over him talked in a soft clear voice to his dying father: "Your Excellency, the supreme moment has come; for twenty-five years you have fought the holy battles of the Lord sacrificing your whole life. Renew again the offering of yourself now! Very shortly you will go to receive the crown promised to those who have left everything for God."

The apostle could not talk but was perfectly conscious. "His great, noble features," continues Father Bouchard, "brightened with celestial joy and showed us heaven to which he was looking with eager love. . . ."

After vomiting abundant blood he felt relieved. He recomposed himself serene and amiable as a child. Six minutes later, the passion of the martyred Bishop was over. It was October 10, 1881, 10 P.M.

"His death has plunged us into the most tremendous sorrow, but the certainty that our Father is in heaven sustains us. We missionaries, priests, brothers, and sisters, present at the passing of "The Just" have repeated his war cry: "Africa or Death!" So concluded Father Bouchard.

As soon as the children of the mission-school were told of the Bishop's death something not quite foreseen and certainly indescribable happened. All as one, burst into such a wild, desperate crying, so loud and prolonged that very soon all Khartoum knew of the death of the "Mutran es Sudan"—the

Bishop of the Africans. The children stretching their arms towards the Bishop's room kept crying the refrain: "Oh, our Father, oh, our Father!"

In no time all the yards and the surroundings of the Mission were crowded with people of all races and religions who in their oriental style started a very loud mournful crying of their own.

Friends and other persons, in gratitude for all the Bishop had done for them, arranged on the same night a beautiful bier in the garden where Comboni was laid out in his episcopal vestments. All night and the following morning people kept coming to weep and lament their common father and benefactor.

Because of the very hot and humid climate, burial in the Sudan has to follow almost immediately after death. At eight in the morning the blessed remains of the Bishop of Central Africa were taken into the chapel for the Solemn Office and High Mass. All the authorities were present with Governor General Rauf Pasha, and the consuls of Italy, Austria, France and England, and also all the government employees and the two brigades of troops stationed at Khartoum.

The crowd filled the chapel and the whole enclosure of the mission. Some were even standing or sitting on the surrounding walls and on the roofs of the buildings. Many were in tears, especially the

poor and the slaves, covering their heads with dust
bursting into loud, desperate sounds of mourning:
"If our Father is dead, who will help us?"

Before the burial, the Austrian consul said a
few words of farewell to "his friend and to the
Angel of Africa." None of the missionaries had the
strength to speak. The supreme sorrow held them
almost paralyzed. It was going to take them more
than a few hours to convince themselves that what
had happened was really true.

The coffin was carried by the fathers, the European consuls and some of the local authorities back
to the mission garden where Comboni was buried
next to Father Ryllo, S.J., the first Pro-Vicar Apostolic of Central Africa.

One of Comboni's biographers wrote: "Comboni had asked for either 'Africa or Death' but actually he had both." How true! Young Pimazzoni,
whom we have already quoted so much, sent a report to Verona on the death of his most beloved
Father which opened with these words: "Africa
or Death! It was the most eloquent and spontane-
ous expression which, born deep in his heart, he
showed by his voice and confirmed by his noble
actions. We know today that he is like a bright
star shining in heaven; while we his children, the
Church, science and all Africa. . . weep unconsolab-
ly for him. . . The teachings and the heroic actions
of the long-mourned dear Apostle must be the mod-

el and the inspiration for anyone, really called, who follows that vocation of a missionary for Central Africa."

All Europe, caught by surprise by the sad news, remained shocked and wondering about the future of Central Africa.

Pope Leo XIII raising his lean arms towards heaven exclaimed: "Poor Africa, what a loss!" With his arms crossed on his breast and his eyes filled with tears, his gaze remained fixed on the Crucifix for a long time.

Telegrams and letters poured in from all over Europe to Cardinal Canossa, as the protector of Comboni's Institutions. Cardinal Simeoni, Prefect of Propaganda Fide, wrote: ". . . We see how God calling Comboni to Himself wanted to reward the many years of apostolic, hard work spent by him in the Mission of Central Africa. His death, however, is the most serious loss for the Mission. . . His lively faith, ardent zeal and energetic character; his most burning desire to spread the light of Faith and civilization among the primitive people of Central Africa; his vast knowledge of their country, of their customs and of the many languages spoken by them, had made him most fit for that particularly difficult Mission. . . ."

Many solemn Requiem Masses were celebrated for him in many cities by Cardinals and Bishops. In the cathedral of Verona, the day of the celebration, people started to assist at Mass from the early morning. Many, many priests of the diocese celebrated the Holy Sacrifice that day in the cathedral, as a token of affection to their beloved friend and martyred apostle of Central Africa.

Many commemorations were also held in seminaries, houses of study, and academies. The theme was always the same: "He lived and died for Africa, only and entirely!"

Comboni himself one day had written to a friend: "Keep very clearly in mind that Comboni can live only for Africa and for whatever has to do with Africa!"

He had been an easy prophet: he did just that.

The Korosko desert crossed so many times by Comboni
and his Missionaries

The famous "Comboni's tree" under which he wrote
hundreds of letters

First Mission Station at El Obeid, Sudan

Mother Mary Bollezzoli.

First Church of the "model village" of Malbes, Sudan

Comboni and Daniel Sorur, the second of his African priests

Mission Station at Delen, Sudan

Cairo—Bishop Comboni with some of his missionaries and
lay helpers. At Comboni's left is Father Taggia, O.F.M.,
of Old Cairo

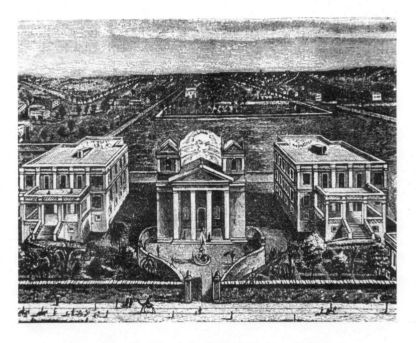

Cairo—The Church of the Sacred Heart and the two
buildings for boys and girls—one of the last
works of Comboni

The garden of the Mission of Khartoum, Sudan,
a few months after Comboni's death

4

CUT FLOWERS

MOTHER AND SON

"I love you not for your handsome appearance, but for your great heart and for the love of God that is burning in it," so Bishop Massaia had written to Comboni.

At the end of this hasty review of his life, there can be no doubt in our mind that in Comboni's great heart there was really an exceptional love for God.

We have to add that this intense love in Comboni materialized in an eminent degree specifically towards the Most Sacred Heart of Jesus and His divine Mother. We might say that, in order of time, Mary came first. He learned on his very mother's knees how to love the beautiful Lady and her little Son; he learned how to pronounce her name and His name before any other word: actually the two had always gone together since. His theological studies greatly deepened the idea of this union and he rejoiced at the truth that the sweet Virgin Mother is so close to her Son that God thought of them together since eternity and she existed only in order to be His Mother.

Long before school age, it was kind of matter-of-fact for him to kneel down and pray all alone in church at the altar of the divine Mother, before her image.

His burning love for the Sacred Heart, clear
and definite, is naturally of a later date. We might
say that Comboni is a son of his times. We recall
how his famous "Plan for the Salvation of Africa"
was inspired and written by him during the triduum in preparation of the beatification of the great
confidante of the Sacred Heart, Margaret Mary
Alacoque.

To smooth the way for a favorable acceptance
of his pressing "Postulate" for Africa, Comboni had
sent a circular letter in Latin to all the Fathers of
the First Vatican Council. This letter, very significantly, was dated "June, 1870—Feast of the Most
Sacred Heart of Jesus!"

Comboni also encouraged and directed Miss
Marie Deluil Martiny of Marseilles, France, in her
vocation as the foundress of the Daughters of the
Sacred Heart and the Apostle of the Guard of Hon-
or to the Sacred Heart. Comboni spoke of her to
Pope Pius IX who in a transport of joy blessed the
whole idea.

Mother Marie Martiny kept in her heart as an
answer from heaven what Father Daniel had once
told her: "Spread everywhere the 'Guard of Honor'.
I tell you so because I feel in my heart something
about this idea. You have a mission to fulfill, of
which you have to consider yourself unworthy, and
yet you ought to convince yourself that you have the
secret of it!"

His intellectual and spiritual life matured together with these two great loves: Jesus and Mary. We may affirm that we cannot find an instance where Comboni does not mention the Son and the Mother together at least once in all his letters and sermons.

When in February, 1865, in Paris, he learned that in Verona somebody was plotting to expel him from Father Mazza's institute, he wrote to his dear Father Briccolo: "I can see how having been charged with very important and delicate tasks, though still rather young, having traveled very much and very often, having been all alone in foreign countries with only God as my witness.... all this can give a pretext to those who don't like me for raising doubts and suspicions about my conduct ... but God who is the witness of my actions, of my thoughts, and of my heart, this dear and amiable Jesus, will take care of defending me, or of giving me strength to be able to suffer. I take your advice, therefore, ... I will not defend myself... I offer myself to Jesus Crucified and to the Queen of Martyrs and I will always have the greatest gratitude for those who persecute me and I will always pray for them.... It is a good sign if God allows us to suffer ... storms are necessary to make our heart stronger. With God's grace I will always accept affliction and humiliations. Jesus suffered, Mary suffered, St. Paul and St. Francis Xavier suffered ... let come whatever God wills: I will always bless the Lord."

And again later on, "I have to confess that my heart never felt so closely bound to Jesus and Mary as now. In the terrible uncertainty of my future I feel immensely happy in being a Catholic and a priest, and I can so clearly see how God is infinitely good and never abandons those who trust in Him ... oh, how good are Jesus and Mary! ... I thank with all my soul the Sacred Hearts of Jesus and Mary for giving me the honor and the fortune to drink this bitter chalice ... I bless a thousand times those who gave me this cross and I will always pray for them. ..."

One day in Brescia he was showing the map of Central Africa to Mrs. Elizabeth Girelli and asking her if she could measure that immense country and count the many primitive tribes, all pagan yet, living there.... "But," he concluded, "the Heart of Jesus is bigger than all Africa and in Him there is room for everybody!" And again: "The Heart of Jesus will convert Central Africa and we will all die to succeed in it!" To Father Sembianti, the Rector of his missionary seminary: "The sweetest Heart of Jesus be always the center of communication between you and me." "Our Lady of the Sacred Heart is the Mistress of the Heart of Jesus."

When in 1871 he was planning to make his trip to the United States, he manifested the idea to Bishop Canossa: "Before May is over, during which I have been begging our Mother, the Queen of Africa, herself, to take care of this enterprise, I come to ask your advice. . . ."

In 1871 he wrote: "And when we will be in heaven we will keep bothering Jesus and Mary so much that they will be forced to work miracles for Africa and send there many apostles like Paul and Francis Xavier so that as soon as possible the millions of my Africans may all be converted."

"O Mary, after Jesus, you are all our hope. . . . After Jesus, you are everything for us." (December 8, 1875)

The whole of Comboni's life was a living consecration to the Heart of Jesus and His Mother. All his apostolic enterprises bear the characteristic mark of this same burning love; all were expressly consecrated to the *two Great Hearts*:—the Missionary Societies he founded, his Missions, his main institutions in the Missions.

He directed that the consecration of Central Africa to the Sacred Heart be renewed every First Friday at the closing of the Holy Hour of Reparation. His clear and so theologically deep idea on the concept of consecration appears from his letters to Father Ramiere, S. J., the famous apostle of the Sacred Heart.

The main sources for Comboni's greatest loves were the Holy Sacrifice, the Divine Office, and the Holy Rosary.

Many witnesses testify that his "was the Mass of a Saint." Daily on the altar, by direct contact with the open Heart of Jesus, the great apostle was drawing that mysterious fire for the most abandoned souls of all, which was inexplicable to his contemporaries and that consumed him too soon while still fighting on the advanced front-lines of the Church.

In the celebration of the Divine Mysteries he was neither too long nor too short. His preparation was very accurate and his thanksgiving rather lengthy—at times even one hour. During this precious time when all his spiritual resources were refreshed he most definitely did not want to be disturbed, unless it were for a sick-call. Charity, of course, first. When traveling he never made others wait; he took care, however, to explain: "Yes, we can go. I will have plenty of time to make my thanksgiving on the camel."

Comboni had the same care and heartfelt devotion for the official prayer of the Church, the Divine Office. Often he was seen walking in the garden alone or with some missionary, and it was quite evident that his mind was completely absent from all things around him. How he felt the truth—that actually the Church was praying in him. But Comboni was a typically practical man, that is why in an equatorial climate he would prefer the garden to the little, incredibly hot church. Under the trees he could pray better and that was the whole point.

Even in his long trips on camel-back he always managed to say his breviary. Only in exceptional cases, when leaving too early or arriving too late, he substituted it with other prayers. In sickness also he never dispensed himself unless in a case of real physical impossibility. As a missionary Bishop he had ample faculties from the Holy See in this matter also, and certainly he did use them generously for his missionaries, but as for himself he thought quite differently. He was most probably alluding to this practice of his when one day talking to his missionary sisters he said: "Look how hard it is to avoid the criticism of the world: I have been accused of not saying my breviary when the truth is that I always say it, even if I am with fever!"

One of the missionaries who was crossing the Korosco desert with him in 1878, remembered how, after seventeen hours on camel-back, under a scorching sun they stopped at last for some rest. It was night. Comboni wanted all his missionaries to lie down, while in a corner of the hut by the light of a candle he was trying to recite the Divine Office of the day in honor of St. Benedict. He had a special devotion for him because he was the titular saint of his native parish of Limone and the patron of a monastery that was helping him so much with prayers, sacrifices, and donations. The hot wind of the desert was blowing so hard that he had to screen the candle with his body to keep it lit. But he managed to finish it with all his usual devotion.

As for the Rosary, he said it every day with visible loving transport. Somebody once remarked that at the end he was adding too many prayers to too many saints. "Well," he smiled, "I have so many needs that I have to bother them all a little." Only heaven knows how many rosaries he had said in all his traveling, especially when he was alone. A continual contact with his heavenly Mother gave him strength to keep going, even when he felt so much like stopping and giving up.

He was so firmly convinced of the need for prayer because he was equally convinced of the absolute necessity of the help of God. He loved God. He loved prayer and his friends were those who had the same love. If he wrote to his priest friends in Verona he did to "those who prayed." At Prague he would recommend the Poor Clares of Verona to the Infant because "I know how much they pray for us." If the nuns of Salisbourg did not write he was not worried because "they think and pray for Central Africa."

"With prayer and faith—not praying only with words, but with the fire of love—thus the African Institutions were founded."

"MY BURSAR"

To say that Bishop Comboni dealt with St. Joseph only and exclusively in terms of money is not correct. How many times in his trials he repeated: "Jesus will help me; the Virgin Immaculate and St. Joseph will help me."

To this "most holy triad" he entrusted himself and all his works. He often said: "Strong in these three treasures, we will not fear the whole world and hell with it."

In 1863, Pope Pius IX sent Father Comboni to Dresden, Germany, to take a boy from his protestant relatives. The boy's mother had become a Catholic and her relatives always stubbornly refused to give back her son to her. Father Comboni had a very hard time. For many long hours he had to talk and argue, but finally he succeeded in taking the boy away with him. He was happily walking towards the railroad station when a stranger approached him and said briefly: "Please don't go this way, somebody in this street is waiting for you to kill you."

Comboni started to thank him but the unknown person was already gone. Comboni always believed that his benefactor on this occasion was St. Joseph himself, or an intermediary because he had put that trip under his protection and he did not then have any friend in Dresden.

It is a fact, however, that the typical task entrusted to St. Joseph by Comboni was to provide for material needs. We have already seen how St. Joseph never failed him money-wise. He officially had elected him as his Bursar. He confidentially called him "Joe, my Bursar" and used to say that "He was poor in order to provide for others"; that "he was always young, always had a generous heart and a good brain, loved his Jesus and the interests of His glory"; that "he never went bankrupt, but was a good administrator, perfectly honest . . . the most honest of all."

In 1879, while saying good-bye to some of his missionary sisters who were leaving for Africa, he put his hands in his pockets and gave them the little money he had. "Take it, you might need it; it is all that I have right now, but I will go pull the beard of St. Joseph."

He repeated very often that "He was going to get everything from the beard of St. Joseph . . . that in his beard there were millions!"

During the period of the terrible famine of 1878, we remember how he insisted on the same idea and, two months later, again writing to Propaganda Fide in Rome, with equal certainty he stated: "My sweetest Bursar, St. Joseph, will send me the hundred thousand francs necessary to balance my budget."

This boundless confidence in the heavenly Bursar he always tried to instill in others also. Once he wrote to the Rector of his seminary in Verona: "Have a true, sound and total trust in St. Joseph and don't worry a single second about money and material things . . . just take care of the Kingdom of God and His justice, as you are doing so wonderfully to my great comfort. . . .".

One of the most striking examples of his own rewarded trust occurred in Verona, in the afternoon of fall, 1877. The baker was at the door of the seminary for the African Missions and insistently asked to talk with the Bishop. Comboni knew, of course, what it was all about, so as he met him in the parlor he just told him that he was well aware that the seminary owed him a few thousand lire for bread, but that he did not have a penny. "Why, don't you come back tomorrow?"

The poor man quieted down and gave in with resignation. He had come so many times, that he could come once more as well.

Back in his room the Bishop started to talk with the statue of St. Joseph he had on his desk: — "You know what kind of predicament and deeply embarassing situation I am in, . . . well, if you don't listen to me, I'll turn your statue and will never pray to you anymore. Now it is up to you to decide."

Not even an hour had passed after this Comboni-style prayer before the doorbell rang again. It was a gentleman who wished to see the missionary

Bishop. "Your Excellency, please don't ask me who
I am or who sent me here; I have simply to give you
this letter!" He kissed the Bishop's ring and off he
went.

Comboni opened the letter and found in it some
few thousand lires. He immediately called the baker
who indeed was there in no time. "Here is your money," said the Bishop. "Now you are satisfied, are
you not?"

"I don't understand, your Excellency. One hour
ago you did not have a penny and now. . . ."

"That is right; before I couldn't and now I can!
St. Joseph never fails."

"But this is a miracle. . . ."

"It certainly is!"

"Then I want to do something myself for your
missions," and the baker gave the Bishop a nice
donation.

"Thank you! You see? St. Joseph is coming
again. . . ." said Comboni smiling.

The unique confidence of the missionary Bishop in dear St. Joseph was something very conta-
gious. Comboni never failed to tell everybody to go
to St. Joseph for anything, with absolute certainty of
obtaining it.

One day Sister Catherine, the Superior of the
Franciscan Sisters in Cairo, Egypt, told Comboni
that she did not have a thing to feed her dear
orphans.

"Well," was the answer, "just talk to St. Joseph about it and be sure to be strong with him. Tell him that you will turn him against the wall if he does not provide." And the good Sister did exactly that.

At noon when the church bell was ringing for the Angelus, the orphanage doorbell was ringing also. The doorkeeper ran to open the door and there was an old man with a carriage loaded with groceries.

"Here is a letter for the Superior," said the old man. When the doorkeeper came back the old man was gone. But not the carriage loaded with the groceries. Well, St. Joseph just could not have failed!

The whole life of Comboni had passed under the sweet care and protection of the loving Virgin Father of Jesus. The last birthday of Comboni—March 15, 1881—was to be marked by his usual boundless confidence in St. Joseph and by the same prompt response of the dear Saint to the requests of his beloved protegé. At the closing of a dinner, given in his honor by his missionaries and the civil authorities of Khartoum, Comboni had thanks of appreciation for all, and, quite naturally, he soon began to speak about his beloved Africa. In making a kind of report, he noticed how the financial point was unquestionably the most bleak. Far from showing any kind of worry, to the surprise of all, he bluntly stated that by the end of the semester the huge debt would be paid. Looking slowly around in his guests' very eyes he added very clearly and distinctly: "Gentlemen, I assure you that by August, St. Joseph will bring to my desk 60,000.00 francs. I wish to repeat: 60,000.00 by August!"

His intimate friends applauded most cordially; some of the "civil authorities" looked at each other as if it were a joke to laugh at, or what. . . . But the situation reached the climax when Comboni, without losing a minute, stood up again with a paper in his hand: "Dear friends, I ask you to kindly countersign this agreement between me and my heavenly Procurator. We two aren't used to joking on important matters such as this; the signing of the paper is called for by his honor and mine as well."

All signed extremely delighted. All, but one, who could not help seeing in the affair a kind of tempting of God. To the credit of this "doubting Thomas" we have to add that when in August the exact amount of money agreed upon came, he indeed changed his mind about the rather "strange" ways of Comboni and his terrific Procurator.

"ADORABLE PONTIFF AND KING..."

The first Vatican Council was approaching and we recall the letter Comboni wrote from Cairo to Pope Pius IX assuring him of his love and devotion despite his being so far away.

"We can say in all truth that every day you become for us something more sacred, a marvel more prodigious, a love more strong . . . your name is the sweetest of all our memories, your image the most pleasant of our companies, your history the most frequent subject of our conversations. Every day we pray for you, speak of you, think of you; with you we suffer, and night never comes without a sign and a prayer for you by us and our African children."

"Adorable Pontiff and King, may heaven save you for many years to come. We protest our determination to accept with perfect obedience of will and intellect whatever decisions the Council may take, as express revelations from God, ready to teach them and to defend them even with our blood and our life."

Going briefly through Comboni's life we saw how these were not only words. His whole life proved in word and in deed that he literally was "sold to the Holy See."

To a friend he wrote: "We must cling to the Holy Father."

In 1865, in his unconditional love for the Pope, he preferred to go to Verona from Bologna via Milan rather than to give in one inch to the anticlericals. That meant to prolong his trip three or four times the original distance, but he did not hesitate a second.

"What a pleasure to suffer for the Pope," he wrote to Mitterrutzner mentioning the incident. "It is a pleasure which compensates for all troubles."

During the fall of the preceding year, Cardinal Barnabo had asked Father Comboni to take for a visit to Pius IX a young Mohammedan man and a Jewish boy, a cobbler by trade, both recent converts to the Faith. Comboni was very happy to do it. The following Sunday together with Baron Visconti and Monsignor Place he was invited to dinner by Count de Sortiges, French Ambassador to the Holy See. During the dinner the talkative ambassador told his friends that he had asked Pope Pius IX, on behalf of Napoleon III, for the recently baptized Jewish boy, in order to give him back to his Jewish parents and that the Pope had answered with an emphatic "No!"

"What folly, what fanaticism on the part of the Pope to deny the emperor something so insignificant as a little cobbler!" concluded the ambassador.

Monsignor Place and Baron Visconti tried to defend the Pope.

"And what about you, dear Father?" the Frenchman had the unhappy idea to ask Comboni.

"I beg your pardon, dear ambassador," came the prompt reply, "but don't you see how the Holy Father is a perfect imitator of Jesus Christ Who would have shed his blood for even a single soul? What a splendid gesture! To me this sublime action of the Supreme Pontiff is an expression of all the poetry of our Holy Faith. Yes, dear ambassador, this refusal of the supreme authority on earth to the most powerful emperor is worthy of the admiration of the whole universe and it shows the indomitable courage of Pius IX. To me it is the unequivocal proof of the great soul, apostolic zeal, and superhuman charity of the greatest Pope of our times, Pius IX, whom I extremely admire."

All applauded the orator. The dear ambassador had lost all his wit by now and tried to cover his embarrassment with a forced smile simply adding, "Oh, you are a poet, my dear friend."

Let us not think, however, that Comboni was with the Holy See only when everything was rosy and easy. For Propaganda Fide and the Holy See he gave up his most cherished dreams, such as his acceptance of the mutilation of his "Plan for the Salvation of Africa" and the complete cutting-off from his mission territory of all the virgin tribes of the interior. He bowed to Rome and helped in whatever way he could the missionaries sent there.

Literally for Comboni what was not with the Pope was against him and he did not want to have anything to do with it.

When in May, 1868, the anticlerical Italian government, which was persecuting the Pope and the Church in so many ways, offered him the cross of Knight of the Kingdom, "for his scientific and humanitarian achievements," he contemptuously refused it. Cardinal Barnabo wrote to him on June 4th not to accept it, but the message arrived too late because Comboni from Cairo had already rejected it on May 25th. In a strong letter to the Italian government he stated in no uncertain terms that: "As a priest and as a Catholic missionary I am ready to sacrifice my life a thousand times to defend even the least truth and declaration coming from the Vicar of Christ."

He asked Bishop Canossa to return the Knighthood diploma for him and he published in the paper "Catholic Unity" this solemn declaration: "I, Father Daniel Comboni, Apostolic Missionary, to the immortal Pontiff and King, the great Priest of the new Alliance, the Successor of the Apostles, the Prince of the Bishops, the Shepherd of Shepherds, Pius IX; I salute you, most holy Father, the true friend of humanity, the glory of the Supreme Pontificate, the Protector of justice and right, the Savior of modern society, the champion of universal civilization, the terror of the multi-headed monster of impiety. Impart, most Holy Father, your thaumaturgic blessing

over me, your humble son, over my dear missionaries, over my institutions for the salvation of Africa. It is better to suffer with you than to rejoice with
the world! Crosses and trials suffered with you for
the love of God are a thousand times sweeter than
the honors of this world and the comforts of the
earth."

And with his article he sent to Rome a donation to the Association of St. Peter for the Holy
Father: "To satisfy my heart and to give good example to the others."

As one of Comboni's biographers said: "To understand the full import of this declaration we
should go back to the European history of over a
century ago." It should be noted, moreover, that
another priest, an ex-missionary, was doing the very
opposite by accepting what Comboni had so firmly
rejected.

When horribly calumniated shortly before his
death, Comboni's great consolation was the fact that
the report was going to Rome ". . . where they decide by the light of the Holy Spirit; where men are
judged for what they are: farmers as farmers, shoemakers as shoemakers, priests as priests, and bishops as bishops. In Rome on the scales of justice they
will weigh my reasons on one side and yours on the
other; and after Rome has spoken, we have to bow
our head and accept with respect the decision either
for or against us. I will be the first to say that I'm
wrong, that I'm an ass, if Rome says that I'm wrong.

I am really happy. Now I am most tranquil and sure that innocence and justice and truth will triumph. . . ."

A few days later, on August 30, 1881, he wrote to Father Sembianti: "Of course, we might now have to change our opinion according to what Rome will decide: that blessed papal Rome which is the providential oasis of truth and justice and which spreads its light over the thick darkness that covers the whole universe."

How very appropriately Franceschini wrote: "He who was saying this was not one who had just received the Red Hat, but one who bowed to Rome even in his most dear and cherished interests and was now waiting for judgment on his innocence in a predicament extremely delicate."

He was exact almost to the point of scruple in following the directions of the Holy See and Propaganda Fide. "I have sold my will, my life, and all my self to the Vicar of Christ, to the Cardinal Prefect of Propaganda and to their venerable representatives and I mean to work exclusively, I would say blindly, under their wise guidance and authority. I would refuse to convert even the whole world, were it possible with the grace of God, if in order to do so I would have to go against the authority and the command of the Holy See and her representatives, which is the only source of blessings, and light."

It is only fitting to note here that Comboni's militant loyalty to the Holy See and his deep love for the Pope did not begin with his appointment as head of the African Missions or his consecration as Bishop. As a tiny boy he was taught by his parents how to love and venerate his dear priest. He grew up in a rich parish life where it was held as a crime to speak a single word against the teaching of the beloved Pastor in matters of religion. These basic ideas were matured and perfected in his seminary training and theological studies.

Moreover, as a contemporary of the great Don Bosco, he was brought up in the belief that saints are born and developed in the warmth of an intense love for the Holy Eucharist, the Mother of God, and the Holy Father.

How richly Comboni corresponded to these graces can be illustrated by one striking instance during his early priesthood.

It was October 1, 1860. Father Comboni was twenty-nine and at home in Limone where he had been sent to recover his strength after the first African expedition under Father Mazza. The opportunity for a trip to Verona came his way and he went down to the little port on the Lake Garda to take the first steamboat anchoring there. As soon as he boarded the boat, however, he noticed something strange going on, a kind of big celebration with plenty of food and wine everywhere. Naturally he could not refrain from asking at the ticket booth the reason for all this.

"Well, Reverend, they are celebrating the capture of Ancona." The Italian troops had invaded the Papal States and were already occupying that important port on the Adriatic Sea.

Comboni was seen to pale and stiffen. After a few seconds with a perfect about-face he got off that boat. Shortly after, the signal of the siren was heard and the steamer started moving away. It had barely reached the middle of the Garda when a terrible explosion broke the air and in no time the boat went down in smoke and flames. Forty-four persons lost their lives. A memorial stone on the shore of the lake near Limone commemorates the strange tragedy of that fall, 1860.

"I could not have anything to do," commented Comboni, "with that kind of business. As a Catholic, as a priest, and particularly as a missionary, I thought it a crime even to passively remain in a company that was rejoicing over the suffering of the Pope."

In all truth, his love for the Holy Father had saved his life!

"LET THE AFRICANS COME TO ME..."

"All for you, my Lord. All for the salvation of the suffering Africans." How often Comboni used to repeat these invocations!

"I would die a thousand times for Central Africa," he wrote again and again in hundreds of letters.

In 1878, the Bishop was at Shellal ready with Father Squaranti and others to cross the desert when a Catholic African woman from Khartoum came to him for some help. His hands instinctively went into his pockets but he could not find a penny. Father Squaranti was carrying the pocketbook and Comboni was afraid that he would object; everyone was saying that the Bishop was too easy, that he was giving everything away. So he pretended to have forgotten something and went into the boat reserved for the sisters. Thinking he was alone, he looked everywhere, but all he could find was some coffee and sugar. He filled two or three little bags and gave them to the woman. Then he also provided a camel for her, and this was really difficult. "Oh Bishop," somebody remarked, "All that trouble for an African woman!"

To whom he promptly replied, "Yes, she is an African, and so she is my child!"

265

In Khartoum, he used to celebrate the parish Mass on Sundays and holydays when he would deliver the sermon in Arabic. During his thanksgiving, many poor gathered at the church door to wait for him. For each one he always had a good word and a donation. Waiting for him also at this time were three young men; a Catholic, an Orthodox, and a Mohammedan, for a visit to the poor and the sick of their own religions. One of these guides told a missionary, "He never let us go in with him, but we could see when he came out how happy and thankful those people were."

Quite interesting are some details of Comboni's adventure of January, 1861, when, from Aden on the Red Sea, he succeeded in taking to Father Mazza in Verona a dozen African boys, ex-slaves. Little Bullos, one of the boys, was staying with a good doctor from India and he certainly could have been happy there, but he agreed with enthusiasm to go with Comboni and, not only that, he also persuaded the doctor's son to go with him. Of course, Comboni explained that he could not take the latter because he was not an African.

"What if I paint my face with ink?" the little Indian asked eagerly. "Would you take me then?"

Comboni had the necessary papers from the English governor of Aden for all twelve of the African boys except one, Dubale. Dubale was working for Mr. Greek, an English employer, who was determined not to let him go because the little boy was getting very useful around the office. Mr. Greek went so far as to threaten Comboni to have the governor take the other boys away from him also. Comboni, of course, had never been a man to be frightened by threats, so two days later, he went to Mr. Greek's office and began to talk about almost anything. After an hour of chatting, people at last started to come in and Mr. Greek was on the point of saying good-bye, but Comboni stayed on, pretending to be extremely interested in the pictures on the walls.

Meanwhile, Dubale was there in a corner waiting for his master's orders. But things went otherwise. When Comboni saw Mr. Greek all taken up with his customers he signaled for Dubale to go out, which he promptly did, and Comboni followed him. As soon as Mr. Greek discovered the "dirty trick" as he called it, he became furious and ran to the Catholic Mission where Comboni was and even threatened to beat him.

"Mr. Greek, you disgrace yourself," retorted Comboni very calmly. "On the other hand, if you take the boy by force, I am obliged to accuse you of being a slave trader, and you know very well, Mr. Greek, the English laws in matters of slavery."

Mr. Greek, little by little, calmed down, and even apologized. Later, he called on Comboni, and as a token of their renewed friendship opened a nice bottle of champagne.

Comboni now had all the boys but he did not have any more money to take them to Italy. Providentially, the ship of the French Ambassador for extraordinary affairs in the Orient just docked at Aden. Comboni boldly asked to talk to him, and the result of the first meeting was a free trip on the ship for him and the boys as far as Suez.

In Alexandria, Egypt, troubles again. The chief customs officer, on checking the boys, decided that Comboni's papers from Adens' governor were a plain fraud.

"These boys are Ethiopians, not Indians," he said in a rage. "I accuse you of slavery!"

The boys originally were from Ethiopia, but were declared Indian subjects when freed by the English authorities. The angry officer, however, did not want to accept any explanation and put Comboni in jail. When the soldiers threatened to open his chest with their bayonets, he remained silent and simply smiled. But things were more serious than he thought; in fact two hours passed, and nobody even showed up for any kind of trial. Without waiting a minute longer Comboni insisted on meeting the chief customs officer who came, but who could not be convinced that those boys were Indian subjects. Comboni at last got tired of pleading, and becoming all himself, he warned clearly and emphatically: "If in three hours I am not out of here with all my boys, your big head is certainly going to be shaking on your shoulders!" At these words the officer went away furious, but soon returned and released Comboni but not the boys.

Comboni immediately went to the English consul, determined with his help to take the case to the governor of Alexandria, Rascid Pascia. And that is just what happened. Before the governor, Comboni used all his eloquence and, while with one hand he was accompanying his hot peroration, with the other in his pocket he was passing the Rosary beads and imploring the Queen of Africa for the final victory. After a long discussion, Rascid Pascia took both of Comboni's hands in his and said slowly: "Sit down and rest. I see how these boys are Indians and not Africans bought here in Alexandria. Your word suffices; you are a man of truth and justice," and he offered him coffee and cigars. Comboni, as social as ever, was happy to drink and smoke to Pascia's fortune and health. Coming down the stairs he saw the chief officer of the customs who very humbly bowed to him and said, "Your highness has found justice according to your merit. May your face shine and your mouth pronounce only words of peace; God is God and Mohammed is his prophet."

"If I were a Mohammedan," said calm Comboni, "I would ask for revenge and you know that this would be the end of you. But I am a follower of Jesus Christ, and, according to His precepts, I forgive you with all my heart and forget everything. My looks are tranquil, my eyes peaceful, my mouth has pronounced words of forgiveness."

The poor man fell on his knees and kissing Comboni's cassock exclaimed: "May happiness abide in you and may your father and your mother be blessed. May you see the children of your children till the third and fourth generation."

Comboni smiled at him and said "Good-bye."

In the meantime, the French ship had gone and he had to wait a few days in Alexandria with the boys. During this time an Arab approached the boys and told them that Europeans ate African children. The strangest thing of all was that Bullos, the great friend of Comboni, was the one who most firmly believed the foolish story and even tried to run away. On the ship he obstinately refused to eat. One day all frightened he finally said: "I know why you feed us so well: you want to make us fat so we may taste better when you eat us." He was so deeply convinced of this that Comboni lost many hours with him. Finally, one day he took him aside and asked him: "Say, Bullos, do you know how much I paid for you from Aden to Italy?"

"Very much!"

"And how much does a cow cost in your country?"

"Very little."

"Then how stupid I have been in buying you when with the same amount of money I could have bought twenty cows!"

That did it! Unfortunately, Bullos lived only three short years in Verona. During the terrible pains of his last illness he kept saying: "More, my God, give me more suffering because You died for me on the cross."

Besides his native Gallas he knew Arabic, Indian, and after only six months in Verona he could speak Italian quite fluently. What a wonderful missionary he could have been with his friend Dubale! God, however, had different plans for him.

To soothe the sufferings of the Africans and particularly to destroy slavery was the torment of Comboni's whole life. Going over his biography we noticed how he took the fight into the very heart of Africa where Egyptian officials, even twenty years later, too often acted quite differently from the customs officer of Alexandria.

To a missionary who threatened to denounce the criminal local authorities to Europe came the scornful reply: "We will have plenty of time to choke your voice before it gets there."

Yet no one ever answered like this to Comboni. His name sounded terror in the hearts of the most rabid slave traders. In extreme cases he did not hesitate to face even the highest authorities, who indeed before him had only one alternative: either to bend or break.

One day a certain Salani, having become angry with one of his slave girls, had her bound head-down to a tree and beaten until he thought she was dead. Some passer-by, moved by pity, carried her to the Mission. The sisters took care of her and saved her life. When, three months later, Salani found out that she had perfectly recovered, he came to the Mission and took her away by force. Comboni was out at that time, but as soon as he returned the sisters told him the sad story. Without losing a minute he went straight to the governor, accompanied by one of the boys of the Mission. Along the way he gave alms to two beggars he met in the street. He was introduced into the office without delay and the result of the short, hot meeting was that the governor himself immediately sent his own steamboat across the river and had the young slave taken back to the Mission.

Always, and without exception for Comboni, the Africans came first, because they were the very reason for his vocation, for his entire life.

One Sunday morning, while he was delivering the sermon during Mass, a Syrian came in, and, approaching an African seated on a chair, rudely shoved him off and took it for himself. The Bishop was strong enough to control his nerves and kept on preaching, but immediately after Mass he called for the Syrian and in a tone of voice that was all Comboni's, told him briefly: "Remember that before God, we are all equal. Don't you dare repeat in church anything like that."

He used to say, "Let the Africans come to me, because they are all my children!"

MY WONDERFUL MISSIONARIES

We should repeat here again what we have already observed so many times: the esteem and love of Comboni for his missionaries was so evidently beyond the ordinary. During the last years of his life, he reached the point where he was more a mother than a father to them. This is more remarkable if we consider the fact that Comboni was by nature the authoritative type. His condescension and genuine courtesy were not in the least a product of an inferiority complex, but the exquisite fruit of a sincere love which had its roots in God Himself.

In all his reports on his missions, either to Propaganda Fide or to friends, he unsparingly praises the "heroic work of his wonderful missionaries." From his letters it seems that everything is done by them and he is merely a reporter. The inferno of an equatorial heat, the murderous journeys, the impossible food, the unbearable thirst, everything is suffered by his missionaries, according to Comboni. We know, however, through the letters of his missionaries, like Pimazzoni, Losi, Bouchard, and others, that their "beloved bishop and father" was always first in hardship; never once did he ask from others what he did not first do himself. And yet, particularly in the last part of his life, he could not see himself anymore—perhaps because he did not think anymore of himself for a long, long time.

Probably, the most factual proof of Comboni's maternal love for his missionaries, that fortunately has come down to us, happened at the end of 1878, the "death year." We recall how he sent away, on vacation by boat to Gebel-Tajeb, all his convalescent missionaries of Khartoum as well as the only one who had been spared by the malignant fevers. Meanwhile he stayed on alone as pastor, bishop, nurse, and undertaker as if he had never been sick and were in the best of health! Only mothers can do such things for their children.

Many of Comboni's missionaries owed their vocations to him, and that could have been another reason for their very deep love for him and blind confidence in him as their leader. In all his journeys throughout Italy and Europe the great missionary was looking not only for donations but for "good vocations" as well. His always brilliant eloquence was unquestionably fascinating when the subject was Africa. All his great heart was there in those hot burning words. Indeed generous youths could not resist his inspired appeals.

Many, for some reason or other, could not follow him, but no one could ever forget him after having met him once. Among the most cherished memories of Pope Pius XI, was Comboni's talk in the seminary of Milan when the future Pope was a a student there. Cardinal Svampa could never forget as long as he lived the fiery missionary and his inspired colorful speech about Africa. He would certainly have followed him unless unforeseen circumstances had prevented him.

In the seminary of Brescia, Comboni's visit was remembered for long years. Some young men owed their missionary vocations to him. Father Francesia used to recall the wild enthusiasm aroused by Comboni among the boys of Don Bosco, after one of his unique descriptions of Central Africa.

Young men and young women who had the grace to meet him personally were the lucky ones.

One day in 1872, a country girl went to Verona with her mother just to tell him of her desire to go with him to Africa. Warmed by his irresistable cordiality, both mother and daughter felt at home in minutes. Comboni talked to them in pure Veronese dialect.

"So you want to come to Africa with me?" he finally said to the girl.

"Yes," she answered smiling.

"Very good! Your first name, you said, is. . . .?"

"Josephine."

"Sister Josephine! It really sounds beautiful! What can you do, Josephine?"

"I can cook corn, Veronese style."

"That is wonderful! You see, in Africa one should know how to do almost anything. . . . Then come!" said Comboni, paternally opening his arms.

"Well, let me go home to change my clothes first."

"Why?"

"I cannot come dressed like this."

"You certainly can! What is wrong with those clothes?"

"Don't you see? I'm wearing clogs."

"That doesn't matter! They will give you here a nice pair of shoes."

"But I have to go home to say good-bye to my relatives."

"Here is your mother, Josephine. She can do it for you."

And so, with apron and clogs, the country girl, Josephine Scandola, heavily perfumed with that characteristic hard-smelling, home-made country soap, entered the Novitiate of the Comboni Missionary Sisters. And she became a truly good missionary, assigned to the Missionary Station of Lul, among the Shilluk tribe, where she died a saintly death September 1, 1903. They claim she was favored with special gifts from heaven.

Another meeting, very similar and yet so different, occurred in Central Africa, at the mission of El Obeid. Comboni was in the garden, probably saying the Divine Office as he used to, when he saw a very young boy climbing the wall and jumping in.

"Who are you, little boy?" asked Comboni very kindly.

"A slave of a cameleer."

"Who sent you here?"

"God!" was the firm answer.

The courage and firmness of the little boy really impressed Comboni, who saw in the unusual happening, something from God. The name of the boy was DenFarim Sorur. He was of the Dinka tribe, the famous tribe of giants in the Bahr-El-Ghazal province. He had seen his village attacked four times by the slave traders. In the last one his father was killed, and he, with his mother and sisters, were taken as slaves. After an interminable trip through forests, swamps, and deserts, he finally arrived at El-Obeid where his master's house was next to the Mission. After a year, tired of bloody floggings, he planned to escape. Beyond the wall separating his master's yard from the Mission, he found his salvation. The old slave trader tried many times to get him back but never succeeded. Later Comboni baptized him with the name of Daniel. Then he sent him to Rome to study for the priesthood. From 1877 to 1883 he was at the college of Propaganda, where he ranked among the first pupils and admirably defended philosophical theses before the staff of the college and his fellow students. In 1883, he was sent to Beirut, the climate of Rome being too cold for him. . . . There he remained at the Jesuits' university until 1886, when he was assigned as a teacher of Italian and French at Ghagir, Lebanon. Bishop Sogaro, the successor of Comboni, ordained him a priest on May 8, 1887, and sent him back to Africa, to Suakim, where he remained heroically all alone when the Madhist rebels were threatening the city from all sides. Then for two years, from 1889 to 1891, he traveled all over Europe with Father Geyer, begging for funds and it is apparently due to him that the churches of Heluan and Suakim could be built and a very important property purchased for the Missions at Gesira, Egypt.

"Very fluent in several languages: Italian, French, English, German, and Arabic, he was a real blessing for the Mission. The most promising hopes were had for him, but after taking sick with cough and fever, he died, offering his life to the Sacred Heart for his beloved Africa, January 11, 1900." (Grancelli)

Comboni, like Blessed Justin de Jacobis, the great Apostle of Ethiopia, immediately realized the necessity of the native clergy. He had the consolation of seeing one of his African seminarians, Anthony Dubale, reach the Holy Priesthood.

He used to pray daily for more missionaries.

"I pray every day for crosses, for missionaries, and for money," he said. And also, "My missionaries have to be Cistercians at home, and apostles outside."

The death of one of them was always the greatest cross God could ever send him. After the first shock, he had the strength to raise his eyes in tears toward heaven and say, "Fiat. . . . courage and prayer. . . . Africa or Death. . . ."

MY FIRST LOVE

"Keep very clearly in mind that Comboni can live only for Africa and for whatever has anything to do with Africa."

These words in a letter to Canon Mitterrutzner, in 1865, from young Father Daniel (he was thirty-four) can be called Comboni's own autobiography. Volumes could be written on the Bishop Martyr of Central Africa, but anything new could hardly be added to this autobiography of his. Indeed, as a real genius, in a few strokes he gave us a masterpiece; while as a man of God, he was also making a genuine prophecy.

The whole reason for his life was always exclusively Africa!

We can read most carefully the hundreds of letters he wrote—some short, others even forty pages long. We can study in all details his endless traveling, all the contacts he made, at times with the highest personalities; we can consider very closely all his sufferings and even death; but we will never be able to find any other motive for all this, save the conquest of Africa for Christ.

Comboni is a missionary and only a missionary—this is a terrific glory for him. To be able to understand this fact, we have to remember that the

Africa of the 19th century was the favorite field for European explorers and merchants as well as for missionaries. Slowly, but with deep determination, politics came into the picture. The European 'Powers' began to grab the more strategic points of the still sleeping dark continent, and ably tried to attract to their orbit any other activity, even missionary expeditions, when at all possible.

The great explorer and missionary, Livingstone, in 1858 "resigned his post as a missionary to enter the service of his country, England, at a better pay." (H. Haeck, S.J.)

Even some Catholic missionaries were sincere sympathizers for the interests of their country in this critical period. The temptation was strong and most subtle. In such a particular atmosphere of mixed interests Comboni, through God's grace, was most definitely immune to any weakness. He dealt with so many high-class people, politicians included, but he magnificently used all in favor of his plans for his Africa. Never did the contrary happen even once!

Comboni wrote to Father Mazza from Rome on October 10, 1864, that he was never going to put his missionary activity under any political power. "To the suggestion of Cardinal Barnabo to establish, in Paris, the central committee of the plan for the salvation of Africa, I answered an absolute 'No'." If it could not be Rome, then Cologne was Comboni's choice because that big Catholic city was "subject of a Protestant government" and so there was no danger of any meddling.

And to Bishop Canossa from Cairo he wrote on December 20, 1867, "Knowing very well that the protection the European governments offer to the missions is only an excuse, I keep myself, in their regard, in a respectful and friendly independence."

On March 25, 1873, he wrote very plainly to Propagnada Fide from El-Obeid that "under the pretext of abolishing slavery, England was sending to Africa its representatives in order to realize its plans of political interests and conquest." His only great ambition was "to plant the Church in Africa in order to conquer it all to Christ," and this passion for Africa materialized as we know in the famous "Plan for the Salvation of Africa" for which he suffered and battled all his life.

We have seen how he wrote it in Rome in 1864, during the triduum for the Beatification of Margaret Mary Alacoque. In it he explained that the prohibitive number of young missionaries who had died for Central Africa and led to the closing of the vicariate, did not prove that Africa was "the impossible," but only that the methods used were wrong.

The central thought of Comboni's Plan is that the last word in the matter of the conversion of Africa must be said only by Africa itself; "Africa can be saved by Africa," naturally with the help of

Europe. It was a fabulous work, involved in the training of the Africans themselves; model Christian villages, schools of all trades, catechists, priests, and four universities for the lay leaders of tomorrow. Such a tremendous task called for the generous and total collaboration of all the missionaries working for Africa, under the leadership of Propaganda Fide. This, of course, asked also for the overcoming of all too-personal, or of rather national ideas of any particular religious order or institute. The work of the missionaries, for Comboni, was the work of the Church and all its members, who ought to unite in the effort of conquering the whole world for Christ.

The Plan had four editions: the first in Turin, 1864; the second in Venice, 1865; the third in Rome, 1867, at Propaganda Fide; and the fourth in Verona, 1871. The fact of the many editions proves, first of all, that the Plan had a wide circulation—it was printed in all the main European languages. It also proves that Comboni was not much concerned with minor details; the second edition, in fact, had quite a few changes.

The whole point was to get busy fast and effectively, while avoiding past errors; Africa had already waited too long. Comboni even wrote: "If anyone can propose a better Plan, I will immediately forego mine." (To Father Mazza from Rome, 1864)

To the objections of Cardinal Barnabo the determined missionary wrote on February 25, 1865:

"History proves that all great projects are accompanied by some kind of utopia; how could we expect not to have any in this most difficult one about Africa?" And again on June 30, 1866 to the same Cardinal: "What in the Plan cannot be realized is only minor. If we wait for better times and easier ways to convert Africa, the day of our death will come and we will not have done a thing."

We have to admit that the Plan in the broad lines conceived by Comboni was never adopted. And the main reason was that Cardinal Barnabo did not dare to take the initiative; the Central Committee to unify the efforts of the different institutes remained the stumbling block.

Today, after exactly one hundred years since Comboni's Plan, while assisting at the awakening of Africa, which culminated in the tragedy of the Belgian Congo, we cannot help uttering the old useless complaint: "Too bad that Comboni's daring Plan was not adopted."

History always repeats itself, however, and Comboni comes back to us again in the person of Monsignor T. Cadoux, Prefect Apostolic of Kaslock, Mali: "In the Church we are not Catholic enough and Apostolic, we are not united. We don't have a special kind of organization (The Central Committee of Comboni?) which may assure the efficacy of the evangelization of the world and missionary troops (sic!) ready for action in the proper manner at the critical moment in a particular sector. A kind of

U.N. would be necessary in the Church so as to be able in urgent cases to call up missionaries for specific actions 'en masse.' The encyclical 'Fidei Donum' of Pius XII did come just at the proper time. It was clear and the Holy Father's appeal was urgent. But what has been the result? A meager one! Too many delays, too much competition, too many personal interests that militate against the Kingdom of Christ. How much better things would run if all looked first for the Kingdom of God and its justice." (Cristo al mondo, 1961)

Elsewhere we noticed how the ideas of Comboni of one hundred years ago are in perfect accord with the missionary encyclicals of our last four Popes.

"Missionary work is for all the Church and not for particular institutions only." (Pius XI—Rerum Ecclesiae, 1926)

"The duty of the missionaries to establish a local clergy with its own hierarchy is a most serious one." (Benedict XV—Maximum Illud, 1919; Pius XII—Evangelii Praecones, 1951; John XXIII—Princeps Pastorum, 1959)

And the point of lay-helpers in all the fields of society so much stressed by Comboni, was equally stressed by Pius XII—Evangelii Praecones; and by John XXIII—Princeps Pastorum.

Comboni was perhaps too far ahead of his times, but the official teaching of the Church, some hundred years later proved that he was right.

The French apologist, A. Nicholas, had written to Comboni: "Even if all your efforts were without success, the simple fact that you came out with such a plan, will make you well deserving for the Church and civilization."

Let us not think, however, that because of some opposition from Cardinal Barnabo to his plan, Comboni put on a long face and thought or said, "Let *him* do it!" We will never repeat enough that for Comboni his personal view was not in the least at stake, but Africa. And for Africa he would cease fighting only with death. He once said, "If Rome does not approve one plan, I will write another one, then another one, then another one, and so on indefinitely, but that I give up Africa . . . never, never, never!"

So with the blessing of Rome he started alone: priests, brothers, and sisters in Verona; on the margin of Africa, in Cairo, his two institutions as a training and acclimatizing center; Berber as the linking station between Cairo and Khartoum—Khartoum as general headquarters and El-Obeid the advanced station just behind the front lines, the untouched tribes of the interior; then Malbes—the ideal model village—all African, priest included, his first one, Anthony Dubale—(two African seminarians were studying in Rome). And finally, Delan—the station amid an authentic African Tribe.

"This chain of successive bases, which did cost so much heroism and victims, was nothing but a sample, like a little 'model in plaster' of his great Plan." (Pellegrino, S.J.)

Comboni was ready for the final jump into the interior at the equatorial lakes, but this he could not do for the reasons we already know.

Meanwhile, his superior intelligence and rare gifts kept open for him the chance for a splendid career if he would just accept any of the diplomatic charges in the service of the Church offered to him. But the millions of suffering Africans, for so long abandoned, meant much more than anything else to him. Once he was assured of his vocation he never wavered a second.

In all truth, he could write at the end of his life, "In the course of my arduous and laborious endeavors it seemed more than a hundred times that I was abandoned by God, by the Pope, by my superiors and by all men. Seeing myself so abandoned and desolate I had hundreds of times the strongest temptation (and the advice also of pious and respectable men, but without courage and trust in God) to abandon everything, to pass my institutions on to Propaganda Fide and put myself as a humble servant at the disposal of the Holy See, or of Cardinal Prefect, or of some Bishop. What, however, kept me faithful to my vocation (even when I was accused to the highest authority of twenty capital sins, so to speak, although there are only seven; even

when I had a 70,000 francs debt, the institutions in
Verona going bad, in Africa many deaths, and no
light in sight, but only darkness and I with fever in
Khartoum) what sustained my courage to hold on
firmly at my post till death, or till the Holy See had
decided otherwise, was the conviction and certainty of my vocation; it was always and every time
simply because Father Marani, after a serious exam,
had told me on that faraway August 7, 1847,
'Your vocation to the African Missions is one of the
most clear I have ever seen.' "

This is truly Comboni.

He once candidly confessed, "The first love of
my youth was for suffering Africa." This first and
only love had been indeed the whole reason for
Comboni's very life. For it he suffered and died.

UNLESS YOU BECOME LIKE CHILDREN

"We work for God—let Him take care of everything. Our apostolate is based on faith. Here on earth this kind of talk is not much understood, even by good people. It was understood, however, by the Saints, whom alone we ought to imitate." In these words Comboni, without meaning it, was giving us the basic character of his whole apostolate—an activity not often matched in Church history which at the same time was accompanied by a most amazing, thorough conviction of being good for nothing.

How many times they heard him pronounce the words of St. Paul, "I am a useless servant." And this particulary after things that hardly anyone else had done or ever could do. Indeed such protestations were likely to seem untrue, except that they came from Comboni himself. He sounded so convinced, so natural, that one could not even have a doubt of his sincerity. This amazing man had one of the most large and difficult missions in the world, the "impossible Central Africa," he was founder and only supporter of the institutions in Cairo for the rehabilitation of the Africans; he was the founder and only support of the two institutes for the African Missions in Verona, and yet he could say in all sin-

289

cerity that "without Bishop Canossa," he would, "scarcely have been able to be an assistant priest in the last parish in Verona."

On his missionary travels, Comboni frequently had to pass through Naples where Monsignor Milone was always anxious to have him as his guest. "One day," related the good Monsignor, "I went with a few friends and admirers of his to the railroad station and there he arrived all alone as an obscure traveler, as one with whom the press and reporters have nothing to do. He was carrying his own big suitcase and we could hardly force him to accept some help.

At my residence we opened the heavy case, in which, among rosary beads, medals, crosses, and prayerbooks, we saw the scientific instruments entrusted to him by the Academies of Europe. Among letters and documents from the Holy See I noticed also letters of famous statesmen, great scientists, and renowned artists. One in particular, struck my attention; it was a very fine parchment with the personal seal of King Leopold of Belgium. I asked confidentially to see it. It contained four pages in which the King in a very warm and friendly manner was offering his support and financial help. I congratulated him most cordially. He smiled and said softly, "There is much more than that," and lowering his eyes he added, "to God only honor and glory."

He used to call himself, "A puppet of God—a jackass—a lost sinner."

When, in the beginning, he was working so hard to start all over again, he wrote to Bishop Canossa, "Some see in our work the hand of God and even miracles! I hope God will work them. As for myself, I tell Your Excellency, 'If I am like Jonah, throw me into the sea!'"

And when his life was turning to a close he wrote again to the Bishop of Verona, "I was fifty the other day. I am getting old and doing nothing! Well, good thing were done, yes, in this immense vicariate by the grace of God and God also was so kind in asking the cooperation of my little finger. But He certainly did everything and He also did not allow me to put any obstacle to His work. I must say in all truth with the Apostle, 'I am a useless servant.'" As we see he could not deny the facts, but all was done by God.

This lack of self-esteem prompted Comboni to observations and corrections from anybody with the simplicity of a child. Good-natured as he was, he always took, in the friendliest way and got real enjoyment out of, jokes that others might have played on him. It was well that he had never been fussy in the matter of food; it seemed that he did not even have the taste for it. One day, for example, the soup was so salty that it could hardly be eaten. Some one winked at the others at table and then said, "Boy, there isn't any salt at all in this soup!"

Comboni very naturally put down his spoon and added some salt, amid the most hearty laughter of his missionaries. Regarding another occasion the illustrious Mr. Cipani wrote, "We had a dinner at Limone with him and all our friends, which lasted well over midnight. Comboni was so taken up in answering the many questions about Africa that any time we changed to a different dish, of the many of the exquisite 'cuisine' of Lombardy, one of our party, a real character, kept passing him only plain corn-meal, so that it was all he ate during the long dinner. Finally, someone could not keep serious any longer and everything ended in a roar of laughter to the immense delight of Comboni."

Witnesses related many instances of this kind.

During his stay in El-Obeid he used to sit under a gigantic Baobab tree, soon after his Mass thanks-giving, to take care of his very heavy correspond-ence. There, he was supposed to have his breakfast also. However, when the sister, just before noon, would come back for the tray, she would find every-thing still untouched. At the sad disappointment of the good sister, he would humbly excuse himself in pure Veronese dialect, "I'm so sorry, Sister! I really forgot all about it." And his excuses were sincere, not because he had skipped breakfast, but because the little sister might have suffered for him.

This great man's spirit remained like the one of a child. He was so deeply honest and straight-forward he would hardly suspect anybody. Sister

Faustina Stampais, his cousin, narrated what happened once in El-Obeid. Comboni, loaded with
correspondence, used to eat alone to save time. Taking advantage of his absence, somebody at table
did not hesitate to come out with open criticism of
of him. The good sister thought it her duty to tell
her cousin, who was her superior also. Comboni
interrupted her unceremoniously, "It is impossible!
How can they talk against me, when I do anything
for them."

But, of course, the unpleasant thing at table
went on, so the sister came back again. Comboni
this time was very sharp, "I don't want you to come
to sow discord among us. If you are tired of staying
in Africa, I shall send you back to Italy and, if you
wish, you can go home or join another society. But,
please, don't sow discord among us." The poor sister
referred the case to her confessor who obliged her
in conscience to go back to her "terrible" cousin and
"speak-up." Mustering up the little courage she had
left, she did go back. Of course, Comboni gave in,
at last, to evidence.

He had a genuine horror of even the smallest
sin. He could not understand how a good Christian
had the courage to tell a willful lie. His simple soul
never made or looked for interpretations of Jesus'
words and of His Gospel. He just took the first, plain
meaning of the truth.

That is why God did so often even "move mountains" for him.

FATHER FORGIVE THEM...

"I will always have the greatest gratitude towards those who persecute me, and I will always pray the Lord for all. I bless a thousand times those who contributed toward this cross and I will always pray for them."

These words were not written by a novice in a moment of exuberance of fervor, but by Father Daniel Comboni, respectively in February and April 1865, when he was expelled from the Mazza Institute, without knowing the reason.

Studying closely the life of Bishop Comboni, we can clearly see how his life had not been an easy one as that, of course, of many in Church history. However, at times, at a certain point, the contradictions and obstacles put forward by men against him did reach a rather unique climax.

"In this world I suffered almost anything," he wrote. "And I have learned at my expense that, first and above all, one must have a great love for God, from which only comes real love for our fellow men."

Comboni was anything but a pessimist, or one ready to give up. We knew him well enough. But he was a tremendously positive man; he was able to really love others only and all in God.

When accused, he did defend himself only if it were absolutely necessary. He wrote to Father Sembianti in Verona, "I know that if I keep silent this time, our institutions will suffer, since I am the head of them, so perhaps I will make up my mind to write and defend myself. How many times I did not do it, leaving everything to God, the Protector of innocence and justice."

In his letters we can read between the lines how much he was suffering in defending himself. Even to tell the truth against somebody was too hard for his great heart. And of course, in order to defend himself he was obliged to do just that.

"I confess that it was a real torture to my heart in writing my defense against the one whom I have always loved so much!" And he goes as far as to say, "Oh, how happy I would be if I could say that I am wrong, instead, and ask him to forgive me." This is Comboni. In fact, we might think that he was even going too far in desiring to be wrong so he could be able to humble himself. But indeed, it was much easier for him to ask pardon than to accuse.

And to the one who took him before Propaganda Fide and caused him "agonies" for long months, when the case was over, in Comboni's favor, he promised not only to forgive him but to pray all his life that "God would bless him in his soul and in material things also." Following up words with deeds, he did not hesitate to spend a large amount of money in order to treat his bitter adversary and companions "as splendidly as ever, like a king," as as one of them wrote to Rome.

It is highly significant that in defending himself Comboni never once hid or diminished the merits and good qualities of his opponent and he was always so happy to refer to these same merits and good qualities whenever he could. It is amazing to see how he treated one of his own missionaries involved in the plot of the outsiders we just mentioned. From Cairo he let him come into the Sudan close to him and he went so far as to choose him for his confessor! In a very confidential letter to Father Sembianti in Verona, Comboni gives some details on the matter, which can be even amusing. "In the beginning, Father Rolleri used to find me guilty of sins I never committed (of course this all between you and me). Being austere, hard-headed, subtle and harsh particularly in judging me, it is all to my spiritual advantage that he be here . . . and listening to the inspiration of Jesus, Who is all love and charity, I did not hesitate to choose him as my confessor. And I am very happy in my choice." To the very hard-to-please Father Losi he once said, "Write whatever you want against me; write to Rome, to Propaganda, to the Pope that I am a rascal, worthy of the gallows etc., etc., and I will always forgive you . . . I will always love you. It is enough for me that you remain here in Africa and save my dear Nubans and you will always be my dear son until death." Em-

bracing him he added, "Let us die for our Africans!"
Jokingly he wrote, "If Father Losi, Father Bonomi
(a true gentleman . . . a man without pride who can
obey anybody . . .) and I succeed in getting together
into heaven, (and much more so if Father Rolleri
will be there also, as I hope) we will die laughing
over the very interesting farces we played here on
earth." Indeed, in Comboni's heart there was room
only for love!

There cannot be the slightest doubt that Comboni's heart was beating for all Africa. Still in that
great heart there was a kind of weakness, as it were,
for the regions at the Equatorial Lakes. It was without comparison, the best part of his mission territory
and all his life he caressed, like a golden dream, the
coming of the day when he could have gone among
those simple pagan tribes, away from the influence
of Islamism and the curse of slavery. His missionaries at last could not only work and die, but reap
some fruits also! We have mentioned that the
governor general of the Sudan had offered, in 1879,
to take care of the transportation from Khartoum to
the Lakes, free of charge. However, when his dream
was about to come true, Propaganda Fide detached
all these very same territories from his mission. For
Comboni it was the loss of his "Promised Land." The
blow was so unexpected and so heavy that he felt
like being lost. In a letter to Propaganda Fide he
humbly asked if it were at all possible for him to keep
at least part of that territory, but his plea was

turned down. Nobody knew better than Comboni that there was "Plenty of room for everybody" north of the Equatorial Lakes, (where was also Holy Cross Station and the tomb of Father Francis Oliboni, one of the first companions of Comboni who died there in his arms on March 26, 1858, and was so much the reason for the perseverance in his vocation). Indeed, "plenty of room in hundreds of hundreds of miles." But who knew much of geography a century ago? Of course Comboni knew plenty about it and this was his cross and bitter martyrdom. In all truth we have to say that no missionaries of any society could ever be found to be sent into his territory, (Equatoria and North Uganda) so that in 1894 it was given back to Comboni's sons by Propaganda Fide.

Comboni accepted the decision "ready to give up even Khartoum if the Holy See wanted it so." Another time he had said: "I would refuse to convert the whole of Africa if that meant to go against the wish of the Holy See."

But when Comboni was informed that, at the end, the whole deal was not a fair play, his first reaction was literally the roar of an African lion mortally wounded by a deadly arrow. He sounded exacerbated. Actually, the information given to him was not the exact truth, as it came out later. But at that moment what could a poor bishop know or do, isolated in darkest Africa, his heart bleeding for the death of his missionaries, worn out by a persistent fever, not able to sleep "one hour out of forty-eight"?

"You have to stay here and *taste* our climate for some years to understand something of what Comboni went through," wrote recently a missionary from Bar-El-Ghazal (Sudan). And yet there is no comparison between the Africa of Comboni and the present Africa. The strong personality of the brave General Gordon, governor of the Sudan and dear friend of Comboni, was at the end disintegrated, as it were, by the murderous African climate. The great explorer and missionary, Livingstone, was abandoned by his five companions, his brother included, "It was not easy to get along with Livingstone: and the difficulty became greater because of the cronical irritability and general pessimism, which is the result of the malaria on the white people." (H. Haeck S.J.)

Quite evidently Comboni's spiritual resources were far greater.

His "being sold to the Holy See," his ardent love for God and the cross always triumphed! He could write in all sincerity to Propaganda Fide: "My Jesus, you did make the cross not for a compliment, but that we may carry it. Yes, we will, and gladly!"

And to Father Sembianti, the rector of his missionary seminary in Verona, "But now we have to change our plans according to what Rome will decide; that blessed papal Rome which is the providential oasis where truth and justice abide and which spreads its light among the darkness of the whole universe." (August 30, 1881)

In Comboni's "terrible toothache" as he called it, we see no one's fault, but just the infinite love of an infinitely amiable God who was asking the last heroic sacrifice of His servant before calling him to his eternal reward. Comboni died some months later; therefore, he could never have gone to the Equatorial Lakes. Asking him to give up the land of his dreams, God was just playing another of His wonderful tricks, through which he was giving to the martyred bishop the merits of those missions also! Oh, infinite love of an infinitely loving God!

On his deathbed Comboni repeated again and again in tears: "I forgive everybody!"

His tears, his insistence so as to be definitely sure that he was really forgiving could call to our mind something grave. Perhaps the Equatorial Lakes incident . . . perhaps something else . . . certainly it must have been the last heroic offering of his heaviest crosses to God for his Africa.

Never in his great heart had he harbored the least resentment against anyone.

He truly did live the prayer he always used to say after Mass: "I sincerely forgive all with all my heart."

THE VOICE OF THE PEOPLE

"He did everything like the prophet Jesus." "He was good like the prophet Jesus," thus testified two Mohammedans of Comboni. We have to remember that for them Jesus was only a prophet and that as a rule they hated Christians. For Comboni, however, their esteem was general and sincere.

Governor General Rauf Pasha, a Mohammedan, wrote to him in May, 1881, "I am so pleased over your happy arrival in the Kordofan province. I was told that they were suffering from a terrible drought there. I don't doubt a second that heaven sent the blessed rain because of your prayers. May God accompany you in Gebel-Nuba also and crown your efforts with the best results, followed by the blessings and the gratitude of all those people."

An old Arab was asked by one of Comboni's first biographers what he thought of the Bishop of the Africans. And this was the answer of the good old Mohammedan, "Father, I speak and God hears me and I don't lie, Comboni was a chaste man!"

And again others—"Either for his good works, or for his pure heart, he was like an angel from heaven." "Comboni was pure and chaste. When one says Comboni, he means a man who is perfect, filled with all virtues."

How wise was his policy and how well it paid to "Never let women or girls enter his room, but for any of their problems to hear them in the open."

Besides Mohammedans, there were in Khartoum a good many members of the Orthodox and Coptic Church who had migrated there from the near East. All of them held Comboni in the highest esteem. Here is how the leader of the Coptic Church described Comboni in his colorful, oriental style, "He was, when living here below, innocent, peace-loving, devout, chaste... one who left all worldly things to dedicate himself only to the things of God. He was truthful in his speech; his words being filled with fire and energy. He guided souls by the inspiration of the Holy Spirit. Victorious as the rock of the Faith which is the Apostle Peter, he was esteemed here on earth as a saint from heaven whether in word or in deed. Detached from this world and wholly immersed in thoughts of the life to come, he was given to prayer with purity and devotion. Praying part of the day and keeping watch at night as a hermit, he adored God without interruption. The face of the saint was jovial and from his pure and chaste body came the good odor of Christ. He was truly filled with the Holy Spirit."

If good reliable persons who were not members of the Church had that much to say, we are not surprised in the least when his children loved him as a saint.

He was called the Father of the Poor, the Man of God. When he entered Khartoum after his episcopal consecration, all went out to meet him because "The saint was coming into town."

The African converts loved to receive the sacraments from him, and in all their needs they used to beg his prayers because they believed God could refuse him nothing.

In Europe also, his number of admirers could not be counted and he was venerated as an apostle and a saint. Many used any possible way to get things that belonged to him and which they would not give up for anything.

When crossing the Mediterranean Sea in 1877, a terrible storm arose. The people on the ship "were positive that God was going to save them from shipwreck because the saintly missionary bishop was with them."

We could also quote what the high dignitaries, both of the clergy and of the laity, thought of Comboni, but we have preferred to limit ourselves to "the people," the common ordinary people, either Catholic, Orthodox, or Mohammedan, whose simple voice is always so unmistakably the voice of God.

We would like to close these few thoughts with the picture that Monsignor Grancelli, the first great biographer of Comboni, gave us of him, "Daniel Comboni was five feet, ten inches tall, of athletic form and regular features. His hair was black; his beard black, long, and bipartite on his chest; his

eyes were round, lively and seemed to speak even
before his lips. His forehead broad, his pace and
gesture majestic. Although so dignified as to command respect from anyone in his presence, he was
at the same time pleasant and affable with everybody. His soul, moreover, was all in those eyes of
his, in his gestures, and even more in his words.
When listening to him, one could realize how true
is the saying of the Holy Bible—'Out of the abun-
dance of the heart the mouth speaks.'"

THE APPROVAL FROM HEAVEN

When the Apostles first started to evangelize the world, God intervened, perhaps more often with miracles to help out in the tremendous endeavor. The extraordinary, however, still is, and always will be in the Church.

We like to think of the "extraordinary" as a sign of the approval of God and His powerful, helping hand in the perennial "implanting of the Church."

Since the beginning of the African Church was a very arduous one, we believe possible the special intervention of God, although we do not mean the least to anticipate the judgment of the Holy See on the matter and wish to give to all witnesses only that human faith which trustworthy people deserve.

We recall how trying was the crossing of the desert on camel-back, which Comboni so often endured with his missionaries. At one time even the water ran out. The missionaries, exhausted and half-dead, "entreated their Pro-Vicar (Comboni was not Bishop yet) not to let them die of thirst." Seeing how desperate the case was, and renewing his boundless trust in God, he made a little hole in the scorching sand with his stick, from which immediately sprang water!

Something like this happened in Delen, too, just a few months before Comboni's death when the territory was suffering from a terrible drought and even the well of the mission had gone dry. The sisters called on the Bishop for help. Comboni went to see them and consoled them in his usual paternal way. Then he called the African girl who was helping the sisters around the house, and told her to take a container to the bed of the little creek not far away, dig a little hole with her hands and water was supposed to be there, although the creek had been dry for a long time! The young lady did just that and found there was really water there!

The orchard of the mission of Khartoum was so big and luxuriant that the missionaries always had fruits and vegetables enough to sell in the public market. The date-palms alone—over five hundred of them—yielded an annual income of some three hundred dollars. There were also many orange trees and lemon trees. The secret of all these blessings was a rudimentary, local water pump from which the fertile orchard was regularly irrigated. If only for a short time this precious instrument could not be operated, the prize orchard would have turned into a desert and only the date palms would have survived. This nearly happened once. Because of a terrible cloudburst, the wall of the well gave in. Forthwith the pump, wall and surrounding dirt all went into the well almost filling it. It would have taken probably a month to repair all the damage, but a witness testified, "I was called for this job and Comboni told me to come back the following day. During the night the river Nile came

out of its bed and going into the well cleaned away
all the dirt from it. The water pump could be put in
order in no time. All of us were extremely surprised
and attributed this prodigious happening to the
power of Comboni's prayer."

Another witness deposed, "Comboni had built
the convent of the sisters on the mission ground.
Later on, he had the whole property fenced in with
a wall. It happened, however, that on account of the
wall, the public road became too narrow in the particular spot where the water pump was. The local
authorities one day let him know that the wall had
to be demolished. Comboni did not give any answer. The following morning the wall was right
where the governor wanted it. The inspector was
surprised and asked the people around what kind
of man Comboni was. All answered, "God loves
him very much!"

In the neighborhood of Berber, there was a
marauding lion that really had become the terror of
the city. The terrible beast could kill and rob cattle
from almost any stable. At times it even attacked
men . . . . The whole city was on the verge of despair because in spite of all efforts, nobody seemed
able to kill it. Comboni happened to be passing by
and many of his friends asked him for help. The
good missionary insisted that they should put all
their trust in God and then he promised that the
lion was never going to come back again. And it
certainly never did!

Many also narrated that he, at times, did work marvelous cures.

One witness told one of Comboni's missionaries this story, "The wife of a clerk of Rauf Pasha had fallen from her donkey and broken her arm. She came to Comboni; he blessed her and before my very eyes, her arm recovered instantly—without any medicine. Naturally, the marvelous fact soon became well known and all were saying that Comboni was a man of God."

Again another witness, "A Mohammedan woman had a girl sick with epilepsy. One day, she came to see Comboni and told him, 'This daughter of mine has the devil and is driving me mad. I went to many doctors, but none could do anything for her. Please, have pity on me—do cure her.' Comboni put a medal around the neck of the girl and said, 'Go now and you will never be sick again.' And that is just what happened. After about a month the grateful mother came back to thank Comboni."

Other witnesses testified that he cured many sick people just by making the sign of the Cross over them.

At times God also revealed to him the coming of future events. One day a young lady went to Verona to ask him for acceptance into the novitiate of his missionary sisters. Comboni said simply,

"Not you, but your daughter," and so it happened. The young lady married and her daughter became a missionary of Comboni.

In 1880, before leaving Verona for the last time, he went to say good-bye to his missionary sisters. He blessed and said a good word to each one of them, novices and postulants included. Afterwards, alone with the professed sisters he said, "The last postulant who came into the Novitiate will become the right arm of the superior and eventually will be Superior General herself."

When he arrived in Africa, he said the same thing to the sisters there. Indeed, Miss Constance Caldara, the twenty-year old postulant about whom Comboni had spoken, made her vows and in 1901 became the second Superior General of Comboni's missionary sisters. She was Mother General for thirty years!

During his last trip among the Nubans, Comboni had warned his catechist, Joseph, not to take a bath after a torrential rain. But the good catechist could not resist the temptation and he did. Soon after, he went to him and confessed his disobedience. Comboni became very serious and said, "That bath will cost you your life!" The catechist took sick because of the infection he got from the waters and, very strangely, he died of it.

At times, when Comboni was unable to obtain justice on matters regarding his missions or for poor defenseless slaves, he used to threaten the punishment of God on some powerful person. A witness said, "Such things happened that all believed he had a kind of supernatural power."

Before passing away, he assured his missionaries in panic around him, "Don't be afraid—I die but our enterprise will not die."

After his death, the Mahdi revolution together with other events almost destroyed all Comboni's works. But when the trying years were over, the Institutes of his sons and daughters in Europe started to increase at a marvelous pace. Now they are over one thousand and about two thousand respectively. All Central Africa is covered with mission stations; the whole territory is divided into nine vicariates of which two, the best of all by far are at the Equatorial Lakes, the dreamland of his entire life.

His sons and daughters are working also in Mozambique, Ethiopia, and of course, in the old foundations in Egypt. After World War II another of Comboni's wishes was answered. His sons and daughters took over parishes in the United States among the colored people and Indians, and established missions in Mexico (Baja California), Ecuador, and Brazil.

Missionary seminaries are flourishing also in the United States, Mexico, Brazil, and Ethiopia.

THE LOVER OF THE CROSS

"Comboni's heroic love for God developed in
his heart such a passionate love for the cross that
at times it astonishes us, and the expressions he
used to manifest it make us shudder. He would
speak of suffering with the eagerness of a mundane
person speaking of pleasure, especially so when he
was under a heavy cross." (Capovilla)

"No one ever will be able to contradict us, if
speaking of the love of Comboni for the cross, we
affirm that he had gone literally mad for it." So
wrote L. Franceschini at the end of his thorough
study of some eight hundred letters of Comboni, the
only ones left of the many thousands he wrote. And
the same historian continues, "Cross and sacrifice
are the verse and refrain that infallibly returns in
each and every one of his letters. These two words
are like his signature, his seal. He does not speak
of crosses as one might do comfortably seated in an
easy chair with a book of asceticism in his hands . . .
not at all! He speaks of crosses while actually walking on a path made out of crosses and thorns. He
loves them when others fight and calumniate him.
He wants them when he feels exhausted and all
around him his missionaries fall—overcome by fa-

tigue. He rejoices and thanks God for the cross which is the law of every work of God and he feels honored for this divine treat."

When speaking of the cross, we should have to go over the whole of his life again, because as we have seen, it all grew and developed under the blessed warmth of the cross. Of course, we shall not do that, but limit ourselves instead to a few quotations taken at random from his letters.

On his way to Egypt to begin his foundations he wrote to his Bishop Canossa, "We are going to Egypt ready to suffer much. Crosses and tribulations are necessary to make the works of God go."

When in Paris at the end of 1868, he received the news that Father Alexander Dal Bosco, rector of his seminary of Verona was dying; that the association of the Good Shepherd for financing the African Missions was suspended; his two institutions in Cairo in danger; literally all his works shaken from the foundations; and his father critically ill in Limone, he wrote to his Bishop, "Our dear Jesus is very good—this indeed is a pressing invitation to really love Him. Though in the most terrible trouble, I don't have words to thank God as I would. What if Father Alexander will die? Oh, my most venerable shepherd and father, let us throw ourselves in the arms of Jesus, Who has much love and wisdom and knows how to do things. May His name be forever blessed. Let us trust in Him. I am too happy to be honored with so many crosses, which are the precious treasures of His Divine Grace. Since we work for the most abandoned souls of the world and we mean to work exclusively according to His Will, so may Jesus always be blessed in prosperity and in adversity now and to the end of time. If our Lord lets us have our dear Father Alexander, we will bless Him. If He calls his chosen soul to heaven, we shall have one more advocate in Paradise."

When a few days later, he was told of the death of his much loved companion, he wrote to those who tried to console him, "It is a terrible loss, but we have not lost Jesus and therefore we possess everything. Moreover, this same loss can be a bargain because Father Alexander, who was a little saint, will pray in heaven to the Giver of all gifts Who will assist us in our difficult endeavor. The Lord gave, the Lord took away. May His name be blessed."

In 1870, he wrote to Mrs. Elizabeth Girelli, an old time benefactress of his institutions, "Let us seek the treasure of the cross. The Wisdom of God never revealed itself with more splendor than in the creation of the cross. I will be much obliged to you if you will ask the Heart of Jesus to send me lots of crosses; that will mean that many, many souls shall be conquered to our Faith!"

In 1875, to Cardinal Franchi he wrote, "It is a constant law of Divine Providence to mark the works of God by the cross. It is, therefore, not a small comfort to my spirit, though very weak, to find myself under the weight of heaviest crosses. They fortify me immensely when I think that Jesus Christ saved the world with the Cross. May the crosses, then, always be blessed! The works of God are most solid because born at the foot of Calvary."

It is quite natural that, possessed as he was of such a love, he would take advantage of any occasion to form his future missionaries after the same pattern. During the "death year," 1878, he wrote to Father Giulianelli, "Let us prepare ourselves with prayer, self-denial, and sacrifice for the salvation of a great number of infidels, who cost the blood of Jesus Christ. In sweat and martyrdom, the Church was founded. Please, pray for me each day so that God may help me in all the difficulties I have to overcome to run this vicariate. Everything is on my shoulders; I have to work day and night and, on top of that, I am very often with fever and I pass all night without a second of sleep. To suffer for Jesus, however, in order to give Him souls, is the greatest resource for the heart of a true missionary."

To Father Sembianti he wrote, "Let us suffer a little for the Love of Jesus, because the cross of Jesus, or a little piece of His cross, is more valuable than all the treasures of the universe."

And again, "How many crosses and tribulations to my spirit! But Jesus carried the cross first and all his followers after Him. At night (I very seldom can sleep) I find that I am happy to have suffered much during the past twenty-four hours; much happier than, when in London, Paris, or Petrograd, I was coming home from a big dinner with the aristocracy! Ah, Jesus is more gracious with His dear ones when He visits them among thorns. Roses are for the world."

Some of his missionaries failed him, as we know. Here is his reaction, "I complain of nothing because Jesus humbled Himself to death on the Cross and so I am happy to lick the earth and to receive any humiliation for the sake of God and Africa."

Spontaneously, the lover of the cross brings to our mind the lover of Lady Poverty. Perhaps only the passionate love of Francis of Assisi for Poverty can give us an idea of the tremendous love of Comboni for the cross. The humble Francis had loved evangelical poverty so passionately that he had chosen her as his beloved spouse. Comboni too, one day, early in his apostolate, had chosen the cross as the loving, inseparable companion of his life.

Writing to Cardinal Barnabo, among other things he said, "I am pressed by so many trials that it is a miracle if I will be able to resist under so many crosses. On the other hand, I feel so filled with strength and courage and trust in God and in the Blessed Virgin Mary that I am sure I will overcome everything and prepare myself for greater crosses for the future. I have already seen and understood that I am so intimate with the cross and she is so close to me that I have chosen her, some time ago, as my spouse indivisible and eternal. I assure Your Eminence that with the cross as my beloved spouse and most wise teacher, with Mary my dearest Mother and with Jesus my All, I do not fear all the tempests of Rome and of Egypt. Neither the troubles of Verona nor the clouds of Lyons and Paris. Most certainly, although walking on thorns at a slow but sure pace, I shall succeed in starting and developing permanently the enterprise I have conceived for the salvation of Central Africa, which all have abandoned as the most difficult mission in the world."

It is no surprise that his tender love for the Beloved Spouse kept increasing as suffering increased and as the passion of the martyred Bishop was approaching the end.

In one letter before the last, written to his father from El-Obeid he said, "The Lord may be always with you! I hope He will be always with me also, because I have always served Him as I serve Him now and as I always will until death, among the greatest crosses and suffering and with the sacrifice of my life." (July 18, 1881) Surely here is an echo of the "Cupio dissolvi" of the Apostle of the Gentiles.

In September, 1881, he wrote to Father Giulianelli, "Pray always to Jesus and His Most Sacred Heart for me who am crucified, so that I always may really love the cross and the thorns which will convert Africa."

A few days later, on October 3, 1881, when writing from Khartoum to Cardinal Simeoni of Propaganda Fide, after having enumerated the many deaths of his missionaries which seemed to keep increasing, he added, "My God! Always crosses! But Jesus in giving us the cross loves us. All these crosses weigh terribly on my heart, and yet they give me more strength and courage to fight the battles of the Lord, because the works of God were born and grew always in this manner. The Church was founded in the Blood of the God-Man, of the Apostles and of the Martyrs. All the Catholic Missions of the world that bore fruit have grown in a like manner as the Church; like her they prosper and go on among deaths and sacrifices at the shade of the salutary tree of the cross."

After having recalled that since the feast of St. Joseph, he had baptized forty-six adults, he remarked, "With this consolation I feel in my heart the weight of the cross. Paul Scandi of Rome is very sick; Francis Pimazzoni has fallen ill again (he offered his life in sacrifice to God in order to end deaths of the missionaries and sisters in the vicariate); Father G. B. Fraccaro is critical. O My sweet Jesus! You did make the cross not just for a compliment, but that we might carry it. Yes, we will and gladly."

And finally, to Father Giulianelli on October 4, 1881, "Pray for me in a special manner because I am full of crosses from head to toe. But, Dear Jesus, shall we refuse them when they procure heaven for us?" The very same day he closed his last letter addressed to Father Sembianti with, "I am happy with the cross because when gladly accepted for the love of God it begets triumph and eternal life." These were the last written words of the lover of the cross.

Six days later, on October 10, 1881, at 10:00 P.M., came the triumph at last, and eternal life followed.

From the window of his studio on the enchanted Garda Riviera, the artist Anthony Moro of Limone saw, that very night, and for several other nights after, a luminous cross in the sky in the direction of Africa. He had been commissioned to paint a picture of Comboni, but had not yet begun; this was as far as he could go. The enigma was explained only after the tragic news reached the birthplace of the Apostle of Central Africa.

A luminous cross! Nothing could have been more significant—it was the new celestial edition of the life that had just run out here on earth.

A modern Safari in southern Sudan

Even today old style Safaris are not unusual in Central Africa

A Verona Sister with an old African woman

Verona Sister—Jungle ambulatory, Southern Sudan

Monsignor Vignota, F., S.C.J.—mass conversions in
Northern Uganda

Khartoum Cathedral—one of the many built by
the Verona Brothers

Mupoi Elementary School, Southern Sudan
One of the hundreds built by the Verona Brothers

Bishop Irenaeus Dud of the Jur tribe, Southern Sudan

A little Sister of Mary Immaculate,
of the Acioli tribe, Northern Uganda

BIBLIOGRAPHY

CAPOVILLA, A.: *Daniele Comboni*, 1941.

CHIOCCHETTA, P. - FRANCESCHINI, L. - GASPAROT-TO, P.: *"Archivio Comboniano".* Vol. 2, 3, 4, 1962-63.

CHIOCCHETTA, P.: *"Concilio Vaticano I"*, 1962.

FRANCESCHINI, L.: *"Comboni's Letters"*, 1960.

GRANCELLI, Msgr. M.: *"Mons. Daniele Comboni"*, 1923.

GRANCELLI, Msgr. M.: *"Mons. Daniele Comboni—Rivendicazione da recenti attacchi"*, 1926.

PELLEGRINO, E. & HAECK, H.: *Series "Africa"* Vol. 1, 2, 3, 4, 7, 1944.

DAUGHTERS OF ST. PAUL

IN MASSACHUSETTS
  50 St. Paul's Ave.
  Jamaica Plain
  Boston, Mass. 02130
  172 Tremont St.
  Boston, Mass. 02111
  381 Dorchester St.
  So. Boston, Mass. 02127
  325 Main St.
  Fitchburg, Mass.
IN NEW YORK
  78 Fort Place
  Staten Island, N.Y. 10301
  625 East 187th St.
  Bronx, N.Y.
  39 Erie St.
  Buffalo, N.Y. 14202
IN CONNECTICUT
  202 Fairfield Ave.
  Bridgeport, Conn. 06603
IN OHIO
  141 West Rayen Ave.
  Youngstown, Ohio 44503
  Daughters of St. Paul
  Cleveland, Ohio
IN TEXAS
  114 East Main Plaza
  San Antonio, Texas 78205
IN CALIFORNIA
  1570 Fifth Ave.
  San Diego, Calif. 92101
  Daughters of St. Paul
  Oakland, California
IN LOUISIANA
  86 Bolton Ave.
  Alexandria, La. 71303
IN FLORIDA
  2700 Biscayne Blvd.
  Miami, Florida 33137
IN CANADA
  8885 Blvd. Lacordaire
  St. Leonard Deport-Maurice
  Montreal, Canada
  1063 St. Clair Ave. West
  Toronto, Canada
IN ENGLAND
  29 Beauchamp Place
  London, S.W. 3, England
IN AFRICA
  Box 4392
  Kampala, Uganda
IN INDIA
  Water Field Road Extension
  Plot No. 143
  Bandra, India
IN THE PHILIPPINE ISLANDS
  No. 326 Lipa City
  Philippine Islands
IN AUSTRALIA
  58 Abbotsford Rd.
  Homebush N.S.W., Australia